FOLUKE OLAYELE
PLANT
YOUR
MONEY
SEEDS
Replant Your Beliefs About Money and
Create Wealth at Any Stage of Life.

Contents

Dedication

Dedicated to my son,

Olaoluwa Ayomikun Oluwagbemiga Jeboda

God has His hands on you for a purpose

Seek out that purpose every day

Use the skills, talents, and resources God gave you

to serve Him and to serve others

Then, and only then, will you know great success

Psalms 1:1-3

Acknowledgments

My father, the late Dr. Lawrence Olusegun Olayele, gave me this instruction as I embarked on adulthood: "Remember," he said, "you are not an island to yourself."

Those words have shaped my life. My success is not my own---it is the fruit of surrender to God's purpose and the investment of people who believed in me before I believed in myself, and even still. This book would not exist without the following individuals and communities:

Dr. Lawrence Olusegun Olayele, my father, for surrendering his leadership to the authority of Jesus Christ and leading our family to do the same. I am grateful to him for paving the path of authorship and inviting me to edit his book, The Prodigal Father. He planted the seed of writing in me. That seed continues to grow.

Mrs. Victoria Ayodeji Olayele, my mother, the strongest person I know, whose quiet tenderness and limitless acts of service draw the best people to her and makes them better for knowing her. Thank you for modeling what it means to steward well through loss and still give generously. Watching you navigate widowhood and caregiving has taught me more about faith and resilience than any book ever could.

My family, for being my community, my God selected peoples, and for inspiring each other to excellence as we use our God given gifts to bless the world. Thank you for sacrificing time and attention as I dedicated myself to this book and to building Hand In Hand Consulting. Your patience and support have made this possible.

My Core, you know who you are. You know me to my most intimate, tender, vulnerable core. You challenge me with a graceful firmness in just the right doses. You remind me that I am seen and loved just as I am. You are my safe space.

My Modern Family small group, for being there all these years---letting me serve you while also holding me up. Community is everything. You live out Saddleback Church's mission as a second chance place for grace. We are better together.

Kimberly Chung, for recommending countless books and resources that have shaped my faith and supported me on this journey as a financial coach. You introduced me to Harmon Kong's Values over Valuables. It helped me experience the feeling I want readers to have when reading this book, Plant Your Money Seeds.

Gaeta Training, my time bending coach, Ana, for stretching me beyond what I thought was possible. Meeting weekly to unpack my thoughts has helped me accomplish in months what I believed would take years. This book is a testament to your guidance and the value of coaching. GaetaTraining.com

Minister Sharon Simmons, for planting a seed almost two decades ago in a sermon. It landed in good soil. It was watered and has taken root. I pray that you continue to receive a harvest of goodness in your life and that your children, grandchildren, and great grandchildren receive shelter from the trees you planted.

Financial Advisors, all those who allowed me to ask lots of questions, pick the fruit from your tree, and glean from your wealth of knowledge to determine my footing in the Financial Services industry. Your stories are gold and your heart towards helping others is beautiful.

And to seal the acknowledgements, I thank God---Father, Son, and Holy Spirit---the ultimate Creator, Coach, and Comforter. Everything I have flows from You. Thank You for being the perfect Father, Friend, and Faithful Husband I could ever have.

INVITATION TO CONNECT

This isn't just another book...

It's a safe and honest conversation about one of the most influential areas of your life.

Every page was written to help you understand your relationship with money (past, present, and future) and how it shapes the choices you make.

As you move through these pages and your own money journey, I invite you to stay connected and continue this conversation through the following channel:

Scan the QR code below or visit the link provided.

handinhandconsulting.net/reader

I am committed to sharing thoughtful guidance, encouragement, and practical insights to support you in every season of your financial path.

Continue to the back of the book for complementary resources.

A Word from the Author

In January 2025, I began a journey with a Christian time-bending coach---and the results were so profound that they completely transformed the way I approached both time and money. That experience sparked a desire in me to create similar transformation for my clients.

Bending time allowed me to be fully present as I guided clients through their financial landscape. As my awareness of time deepened, three powerful keys stood out to me. I will pass those keys to you to unlock your finances. I call them the Three C's: Creator, Coach, and Conviction.

1. Creator

The first key to understanding both time and money is surrendering to the Creator.

Genesis 1 describes God's creation of time, space, and matter (which includes money). Time did not exist until God created it. He lives outside of time. Matter did not exist until God created it. That means He ultimately knows how to use it.

God created the financial system. He created trees that bear fruit, and within each fruit, He placed a seed---a cycle of multiplication built into creation itself. At first glance, it may seem simple, yet the entire economy of heaven is rooted in this principle. It's a principle that works. Seeds planted in good ground grow trees that bear fruit. The fruit carries seeds that can be planted to grow more trees.

To truly understand money, we must submit to God as Creator---the source of all systems, abundance, and provision. This truth is the foundation of this book. You'll discover how God multiplies exponentially through the tree → fruit → seed pattern He designed.

2. Coach

The second key is coaching.

Throughout my life, I've had coaches---from my adulting coaches (a.k.a. my parents) to my track coach to my fitness coach to my career coach.

Every great transformation I experienced was the result of guidance, encouragement, and accountability from someone outside of me.

Working with my time-bending coach reinforced the principle that you go further together than alone. Together, we set a three-year goal---and I achieved it in six months. Coaching accelerates growth. I've since applied those same principles with my clients and witnessed remarkable financial transformations.

The benefits of having a good coach outweigh the upfront costs ---every time. Coaching is not about being told what to do---it's about being guided toward who you already are.

3. Conviction

The third key, and the one this book focuses on, is conviction.

Conviction is often called mindset---the lens through which you interpret everything, even when you're unaware of it.

For decades, I made financial choices based on convictions inherited from family, absorbed from culture, or adopted from friends. Then I realized something: I am responsible for my convictions---and I have the power to change them.

This book will help you uncover and reshape the convictions that form your financial life. You'll learn how to inspect what you believe, why you believe it, and how those beliefs impact your financial results.

Your perspective about money will determine the results you receive.

While this book has biblical roots, you don't need to be a Christian to benefit. My goal isn't to preach, but to guide you with love, truth, and practical wisdom.

Everything shared here flows from my relationship with God---Father, Son, and Holy Spirit---the ultimate Creator, Coach, and Comforter for my convictions. The Maker knows the design, purpose, and function of what He made.

When you understand your divine design, you begin to steward your finances from conviction, not confusion. I invite you to take this journey with your finances---one that begins with conviction.

Introduction

Congratulations on taking this step. By picking up this book, you've chosen to travel the money path that few dare to walk---the path of mindset transformation.

I'm confident you'll navigate both the smooth and bumpy terrain ahead with courage and hopeful expectation. But before we start, let's begin with the most important truth: your identity.

You are confident. You are disciplined. You are focused. You are sober-minded. You are a good steward of your wealth. You guard your mind, your body, and your finances with truth.

And if those words don't yet feel true, that's okay---they soon will.

I am Foluke Olayele, CEO of Hand In Hand Consulting. I walk hand in hand with my clients through their financial journeys. In doing so, I've learned that every person's financial path may look different, but the root of their tree---their conviction---is what determines how tall they grow.

This book isn't written from the perspective of examining your tree from the outside. It's an invitation to dig into the soil together.

We'll dig into the roots of your beliefs and follow them through every season of life---from your earliest money memories to singleness, marriage, parenting, loss, and caregiving. Along the way, you'll discover which beliefs produce good fruit and which ones need to be uprooted.

While most financial books focus on results---how much you earn or save or ways to invest to increase net worth---this one goes deeper.

The real key to unlocking your desired financial future is your conviction.

That conviction will guide you through this journey of self-examination.

As you read, you'll gain the clarity and courage to decide:

- Will I stay planted in the same soil?
- Or will I uproot myself and replant in ground that will help me flourish?

This process may uncover unaddressed beliefs, emotional wounds, or cultural scripts that have quietly shaped your relationship with money.

You may feel denial, resistance, or blame along the way---that's normal.

But if you stay the course, you'll emerge stronger, clearer, and more confident than ever before.

So go ahead---dig into the soil. Take a deep breath. We are on this journey together.

What This Book Will Do For You

I wrote this book for people who are tired of choosing.

Choosing between enjoying life now or saving for later. Choosing between paying off debt or actually living. Choosing between being responsible and being happy.

What if you did not have to choose?

Building wealth while actually living your life---that is what I help my clients do. It is the key to enjoying money today with plenty to live off of tomorrow. And that is exactly what I want for you.

Throughout this book, I will walk you through every season of life---from your earliest money memories to singleness, marriage, parenting, loss, and caregiving. At each stage, you will learn how to steward what God has given you without putting your life on hold.

This is not about deprivation. This is not about eating rice and beans for ten years while you pay off debt. This is about building a life you love while building wealth that lasts.

I call this the Financial Renovation Journey. It is not a quick fix.

It is a process of examining your beliefs, building new habits, and creating a system that works for your actual life---not someone else's.

This book is the first step. If you want to go further, I am here to walk with you.

Now let's begin.

Chapter 1 - Childhood

You Were Planted Somewhere

Every tree starts as a seed. That seed does not choose where it lands.

The wind carries it. A bird drops it. A child throws it. And wherever it lands, that is where it grows.

The same is true for you and me.

We did not choose the family we were born into. We did not choose the country. We did not choose the words our parents said about money. We did not choose the feelings we had when we saw them pay bills or count coins at the store.

But those early moments shaped us. They planted beliefs deep in our hearts. And those beliefs grew into the money thoughts we carry today.

This chapter is about looking back. It is about finding the soil you were planted in. It is about seeing clearly what you learned---on purpose and by accident---so you can decide if those lessons still serve you.

Because here is the truth: Where you were planted is not where you have to stay.

The Apartment on 93rd Street

My life in this country started in a two-bedroom apartment off 93rd and Normandie in Los Angeles, California. People called that area South Central back then. Six of us lived in about 1,000 square feet. Sometimes seven, when my aunt came from Nigeria to start her new life in America.

My parents had one bedroom. The four children shared the other. My sister and I slept in one bed. My two brothers slept in another. It was snug. And we loved it.

My mother cooked amazing food. Her Nigerian food is delicious and requested by many. She also loved to make Chinese rice noodles, cornbread, and eggs. Every Sunday after church, we would either eat out at a Chinese restaurant---our special treat---or come home to her cooking. Then the whole family would take a nap. One to two hours of rest. Every single Sunday.

At seven o'clock on weeknights, we gathered in the living room. My father turned on the TV. Jeopardy came on first. Then Wheel of Fortune. We shouted out answers together. We laughed. We talked. It was simple.

It was good.

I never felt poor.

My clothes were clean. My shoes were polished---even if they were a size too big and stuffed with tissue until I grew into them. My mother dressed my sister and me in matching outfits, like twins. She did the same with my brothers. We looked good. We smelled good. We were well-trained and polite.

We had food every day. We had love every day. We had God every day.

That was the soil I was planted in.

The Sacrifice No One Talked About

My father had a doctorate degree. He got his master's degree and PhD in Public Administration. He dreamed of working in government, of shaping public policy, of making a difference in the world.

But when he moved our family to California, he could not find work in his field. So, he took a job as a janitor. He rode the public bus to clean floors and empty trash cans. Later, he drove as a courier, carrying legal mail from Los Angeles to San Diego and back again. He also worked as a security guard.

A man with a doctorate. Mopping floors.

He never complained. He never showed bitterness. He never let us see disappointment on his face. What I saw instead was joy. Surrender. Peace. Gratitude.

I did not learn about his sacrifice until I was an adult. As a child, I thought he loved being a teacher. That was the career he eventually found---teaching fifth grade first at a private school and later for the Lynwood Unified School District. And he was wonderful at it. But it was not his dream. It was his decision.

He chose his family over his ambition. He chose to provide over his pride. He trusted that God would take care of the rest.

My mother made her own sacrifice. She was a teacher in Nigeria. But when she came to America with my two baby brothers, she chose to become a nurse. She worked the night shift---7 p.m. to 7 a.m.---so she could be home during the day for us. She went back to school while raising four children. She led a ministry with my father. She visited families regularly to bring meals and her presence. She cooked. She cleaned. She disciplined us with strength because she knew we were not weak.

There was a season of life when my mother was a full-time wife, a full-time mother, a full-time nurse, a full-time student, and a full-time ministry volunteer---all at once.

These were the people who planted me.

The Messages I Caught

My parents taught me many things on purpose. They taught me to tithe because the Bible said so. They taught me to give to those in need. They taught me to serve others with my time and energy.

But there were other lessons I caught without them meaning to teach me.

Lesson one: We don't have a lot, but we should be thankful for what we have.

Lesson two: We are obligated to give to those who have less than us.

Lesson three: Corporate people who are extremely wealthy got their money in dishonest ways and should give more of it away.

That third lesson came through the TV. Whenever the news showed a rich businessman or a wealthy corporation, my family would comment. "They could use that money to help the poor." "Why do executives get bonuses while workers get minimum wage?" "Those people are greedy."

I remember when the Enron scandal broke. The anger in my home was thick. All those regular people who lost their retirement savings because of rich executives who lied and cheated. The message was clear: rich people hurt people.

My parents did not mean to teach me to fear wealth. They wanted to warn me against greed. But what I heard was this: Being rich is dangerous. Stop before you get wealthy.

A ceiling was placed over my head. And I did not even know it was there.

The Money That Went Away

One of my earliest memories about money is watching it leave.

My parents sent money to Nigeria constantly. Both of my grandparents were still living---my father's mother and my mother's father. They needed care. Cousins needed school fees. Relatives needed medicine. The conversation in our home was always the same: Who needs what? How do we get it to them?

I understood the exchange rate. I knew that ten American dollars meant a lot more when converted to Nigerian naira. I understood that we were blessed to live in America and that our family back home was counting on us.

But as a child, I resented it.

I wanted more toys. I wanted more Christmas gifts. I saw what other kids had and wondered why people I had never met got to decide where my parents' money went.

One time I said something. I asked my parents why we had to keep sending money to people I didn't really know. They were gentle in their answer.

"They are family," my parents said. "And we take care of family. If the shoe were on the other foot, we would want them to do the same."

My parents never asked my permission. They simply did what they believed was right. And I watched.

Our clothes that we outgrew did not go to the Salvation Army. They went to Nigeria. Our extra went to Nigeria. Our sacrifice went to Nigeria.

Looking back, I see it now as generosity. But as a child, it felt like loss.

The Girl Who Did Not Ask

If I had to describe my early money, it would be this: I was the girl who did not think she was worthy of asking.

I remember wanting things and being told, "Go ask your dad." But I could not open my mouth. The words would not come. One time, I walked out to my father and just stood there. Finally, I said, "Mom told me to ask you." I could not say what I actually wanted.

My mother had a phrase she used when we asked for things we could not afford. In Yoruba, she would say something that translated to "Go and take it." It was her way of saying: The thing does not exist. But sure---if you can get it, then go and take it. Look around. Do you see it anywhere? No? Then stop asking.

I learned to stop asking.

My older sister did cheerleading in high school. She was also valedictorian---brilliant and talented. I watched how much cheerleading cost. The uniforms. The competitions. The time. And I decided I would not add to the financial burden.

In middle school, I tried out for basketball. I made it. I quit.

In high school, I tried out for drill team. I made it. I quit.

My reason was always the same, even if I did not say it out loud: I did not want to cost my parents anything extra.

Years later, I went to therapy and discovered where this belief came from. When I was five years old, my mother left Nigeria to join my father in America. She took my two baby brothers with her. But she could not take my sister and me. The paperwork was not ready. We had to stay behind.

I did not get a goodbye.

One day she was there. My baby brothers whom I loved were close by. The next day she was gone. My baby brothers, gone too. I was five years old, and the people I needed most had disappeared overnight.

It took almost two years for the paperwork to go through. Two years of waiting. Two years of growing up without my parents physically present. Two years without my brothers. When I finally came to America before my seventh birthday, something had already been planted in me: Do not depend on anyone. The people you need might leave without notice.

That wound attached itself to money. Why would I ask anyone for anything? Why would I trust anyone to provide for me? If I needed something, I would earn it myself.

And so, the earning mentality was born.

The Moment Everything Shifted

In 1998, I started my freshman year at UCLA. I lived in Sunset Dorm with two roommates named Kristine and Marissa. We were the same height, the same size, and had the same sense of humor. They were Filipino. I was Nigerian. But it felt like we were sisters.

One day, I noticed that Marissa had a car. I asked her a question that seemed normal to me: "How much is the lease payment?"

She looked at me calmly and said, "Nothing."

"What do you mean?" I asked.

"My parents bought it with cash and gave it to me."

I stared at her face to see if she was joking. She was not.

My mind could not process what she said. In my world, everyone had car payments. Everyone had leases. You worked for what you had. You paid down what you borrowed. Nobody just gave you a car.

But Marissa was not a spoiled princess. She was not demanding or entitled. She was soft-spoken and humble. Her family was not rich. They were stable. And out of that stability, they gave her something good---freely, with no guilt, no strings, no obligation.

And Marissa received it. Simply. Gratefully. As if she were worthy of receiving it.

That moment cracked something open inside me. I saw a world I had never seen before. I saw that wealth could be peaceful. That generosity could be easy. That receiving did not make you greedy.

I did not change overnight. But that seed was planted. And it would take twenty-five years to fully grow. Well ... it's still growing.

The House, The Call, The Blessing

Years later, I bought my first house on my own. I worked hard for it. I earned every dollar. Then the time came to move into something bigger.

I found a house that was twice the size of my first one. Twice the payment. Twice the stretch. I was nervous. The budget would be tight. I did not like tight. I liked room to breathe financially.

Before I put down the escrow, I called my father. He and my mother were in Nigeria at the time. But I needed his wisdom.

I told him my concerns. The house was a stretch. I did not want to be irresponsible. What should I do?

My father listened. Then he said something I will never forget.

"I am proud of how you steward money. I value how you think through decisions. But I want you to consider something. My generation---the Christians of my generation---left room for God. We took risks when we knew God was in it. We left room for Him to do what only He can do."

Leave room for God.

Those words echoed in my mind. I had spent my whole life trying to earn everything. Trying to control everything. Trying to make sure I never had to depend on anyone---not even God.

I bought the house.

Shortly after I moved in, I received a promotion at work. It was not a small raise. It was significant---so significant that the tight budget I feared became wide open. I had room to breathe. Room to enjoy. Room to travel and live.

Did I earn that promotion? Maybe. But I fully believe it was God giving it to me. The house was His gift. The promotion was His provision. He opened the storehouses of heaven and poured out blessing.

And I finally learned to receive.

What I Believe Now

Today, I am not the girl who was afraid to ask.

I ask my Heavenly Father for what I want. I tell Him my desires. And I expect Him to give me good gifts---not because I earned them, but because I am His daughter.

I think about Marissa. She received from her parents simply because she was their daughter. She did not work extra hard to deserve the car. She did not feel guilty about receiving it. She just received.

Now I do the same with God. Who else am I going to ask? He owns everything. He is my Father. And He delights in blessing His children.

I believe I am the kind of person who can ask for what I desire. I believe I am the kind of person who can receive joyfully. I believe that God has a purpose for my life, and when I serve others, I am worth being paid for the value I bring.

This is my new soil. This is where I have replanted myself.

What About You?

Now it is your turn.

Where were you planted? What was the soil of your childhood like? What messages did you catch---on purpose and by accident---about money?

Maybe you grew up hearing "money doesn't grow on trees." Maybe you watched your parents fight about bills. Maybe you learned that rich people are evil or that poor people are lazy.

Maybe you learned to earn everything yourself because depending on others felt dangerous. Maybe you learned to give everything away because keeping anything felt selfish.

Whatever you learned, it is not your fault. You were a seed that landed somewhere. The soil shaped you.

But you are not a seed anymore. You are a tree. And trees can be transplanted.

Here is what I want you to know: Your value has nothing to do with money. Your identity is not tied to your bank account, your parents' bank account, or your spouse's bank account. Your identity is tied to your loving Heavenly Father who owns everything.

He owns the cattle on a thousand hills. He owns the gold in every mine.

He owns the stars in the sky and the fish in the sea. And He calls you His child.

You are not what you earn. You are not what you save. You are not what you spend. You are His.

And because you are His, you have wealth.

Reflection & Replanting

Take a moment to pause. Find a quiet place. Ask God to show you the truth about where you were planted.

1. What is your earliest memory of money? What happened? How old were you?

___

___

___

2. What phrases did you hear about money growing up?

___

___

___

3. What did you learn about rich people? About poor people?

___

___

___

4. What belief about money do you want to let go of?

___

___

___

5. What new belief do you want to plant in its place?

___

___

___

Chapter 1 Mantra

Say this out loud:

I have wealth.
My value is not tied to my bank account.
My identity is tied to my Heavenly Father
who owns everything.
I can ask. I can receive. I can give.
I have wealth.

You were planted somewhere.
But that is not where you have to stay.
In the next chapter, we will learn how to choose new soil.

Chapter 2 - Emerging Adults

You Can Choose New Soil

If you are between the ages of 15 and 18, this chapter is for you. You hold something that older people would pay millions to get back: time.

Time is your greatest asset. Not your job. Not your grades. Not your connections. Time.

Because time is the one thing that makes money grow. And the earlier you start, the more your money grows. It really is that simple.

In Chapter 1, we talked about the soil you were planted in. You did not choose that soil. But now you are old enough to choose new soil. You can decide what you believe about money. You can decide what habits to build. You can decide to start planting seeds today that will grow into forests by the time you are 40, 50, or 60 years old.

This chapter will show you how.

My First Job

My first real job was in the 10th grade. I worked for my high school science teacher, Mrs. Annie Williams, at Woodrow Wilson High School in East LA. Not to be confused with Long Beach Wilson. Mrs.

Williams taught biology—the kind where you dissect pigs and cut up animals.

Mrs. Williams hired me and my friend Salena to help organize her classroom. We filed papers, put away science experiments, and kept things in order. She paid us about $25 an hour. We worked two hours a week. That came out to $50 a week.

Fifty dollars a week. That was my start.

Mrs. Williams was more than a boss to me. She became like a second mother. She saw things in me that I could not see in myself.

What did I do with my $50 a week? I tithed and saved the rest.

Because my family had immigrated from Nigeria, I did not have the legal paperwork to open a bank account until I was almost 18. So, my father created a system. He gave each of his children a plain white envelope. On the envelope, he wrote our name and our balance. Every time I gave him money, he added it to the total. Every time I needed money, he subtracted it.

It was simple. It was honest. And it worked.

When I turned 18 and was ready to open my own bank account, my father handed me all the cash. Every dollar I had saved. He was true to his word.

Looking back, I see that my father's envelope system was my first lesson in money management. He taught me to save. He taught me to track my savings. He taught me to trust a process.

That envelope was the first bucket in my financial piggy bank.

The Mistake That Cost Me a Fortune

When I started college, I made a mistake that cost me hundreds of thousands of dollars. I leased a car.

It was a silver Saturn sedan. I thought I was being smart. The monthly payment was lower than a car loan. I got a new car every three years or so.

I loved that new car smell.

What I did not understand was this: when the lease ended, I owned nothing. The car company kept the car. They kept all the money I paid. And I started over with a new lease and new payments.

I leased my first three or four cars this way. I did not stop until I was in my mid-thirties—after my divorce—when I finally bought a car outright with cash.

Let me show you the math.

Today, car payments can be as high as $700 a month. That is $8,400 a year. Over six years, that is $50,400—gone. You paid it, but you own nothing. You don't have a used car to sell to recoup any of your money.

Now imagine if you saved for a used car and paid cash then invested that same $700 a month instead. At 10% interest over six years, you would have about $58,000. Instead of losing $50,000, you gain $58,000. And you still have the car... to resell later if you choose and recoup some of your cash payment. That is a difference of over $100,000.

My car leases easily cost me $250,000 when you count the years I leased, the money I lost, plus the money I could have earned. A quarter of a million dollars—gone—because I did not know better.

You do not have to make that mistake. You know better now.

The Books That Changed Everything

I did not learn about real money management until I was in my thirties. It happened during one of the hardest seasons of my life—my divorce. During the separation, my brother-in-law gave me a book called The Total Money Makeover by Dave Ramsey. That book changed me.

I read it. I listened to it on Audible over and over. I followed the steps. I watched videos on YouTube. I listened to the podcast. I heard people call in and do their "debt-free screams" after paying off tens of thousands of dollars. And I thought: I can do that. There really is a light at the end of my tunnel—and it is not a truck about to run me over.

I loved Dave Ramsey's story because it included God. He did not hide his faith. He showed how God was part of his journey. That gave me hope.

I followed his system. I became gazelle intense. Over the course of two years I paid off $65,000 in debt. I saved a fully funded emergency fund of over $20,000. I saved a down payment for a house. I did it.

Then I read another book: The Automatic Millionaire by David Bach. When I first saw that title, I thought it was a scam. I thought it was some trick to convince gullible people that they could get rich overnight. But I decided to read it anyway. I was trying to see money differently. Maybe I was wrong.

I was wrong.

The book explained that "automatic" means automated. You set up your savings and investing to happen automatically—without you having to think about it every paycheck. You make the decision once, and the system does the rest.

I started automating everything. My tithe. My investments. My savings. All of it happened automatically every month. I did not have to decide each time. The decision was made years ago. The only thing I adjust each year is how much to increase.

Today, I live on about 60% of my income. The rest goes to giving, saving, and investing—automatically. I do not feel it. I do not miss it.

And it grows.

That is how I became a millionaire.

Money Making Babies

Let me explain compound interest in the simplest way I know.

Compound interest is money making babies.

Here is how it works. You put $100 in a savings account that earns 10% interest. After one year, your $100 earns $10. Now you have $110.

The next year, you earn 10% on $110—not just the original $100. That is $11. Now you have $121.

The next year, you earn 10% on $121. That is $12.10. Now you have $133.10.

See what happened? Your money made a baby. Then the baby made a baby. Then that baby made a baby. And it keeps going and going and going.

But here is the key: babies need time to grow. The longer you let your money sit, the more babies it makes. That is why starting young matters so much.

Let me show you the power of time.

If a 15-year-old puts $100 a month into an investment account earning 10% interest and never stops until age 65, they will have approximately $1,396,690.

Read that again. Nearly 1.4 million dollars.

How much did they actually put in? Only $60,000 over 50 years. The rest—over 1.3 million dollars—came from compound interest. The money made babies. The babies made babies. And the babies kept making babies for 50 years.

This is the one thing I wish someone had told me when I was 15. If I had understood compound interest back then, I would have started immediately. I would have saved birthday gifts and Christmas presents and found ways to earn $100 a month. I would have so much more money today.

But it is never too late. And for you, it is not too early.

The Four Buckets

Now let me give you a simple system for managing every dollar you earn. It changed the way I think about money.

I call it the Four Buckets.

Imagine you have four buckets lined up on a table. Every time you get paid, you divide your money into these four buckets or piggy banks.

Here is how it works:

Bucket 1: Giving (10%)

Give 10% to God through the local church you belong to. This is an act of faith and gratitude. It reminds you that everything comes from God and that you are a steward, not an owner.

Bucket 2: Bills (60%)

Everything you earn should not go to paying your bills. Rent. Utilities. Phone. Insurance. Food. Limit your expenses. If you can live on 60% of your income as a young person, you will be rich later.

Bucket 3: Saving (10%)

This is your freedom-from-the-rat-race can. Put 10% into a retirement account or save it to start your own business someday. This money is what will set you free from working for someone else your whole life. This includes setting money aside to invest in yourself. Buy books. Take courses. Attend workshops. Learn new skills. The more you know, the more you can earn. Never stop learning.

Bucket 4: Spending (20%)

This one is mandatory. You must spend 10% of your entire income every single month (repeat, every month spend the WHOLE 10%) on something FUN. Go to the beach. Go to a concert. Have lunch with a friend. Watch a movie. Golf. Get a massage. This reminds you that you are worth it. You are valuable. God wants you to experience joy. The other 10% can be allowed to collect until it amounts to enough for that next big purchase. A car. A house. A vacation. Put this in a high-yield savings account so it earns interest while it waits.

Let me show you how this works with real numbers.

Say you are 16 years old and you make $1,000 a month at your part time job.

Here is how you would split it:

Giving: $100

Bills: $600

Saving: $100

Spending Fun: $100

Spending Planned Purchase: $100

If you are living as a dependent where a parent or guardian covers the expense, and you do not have $600 in bills, that is fine. Keep your expenses low and put the extra into savings or set it aside for a planned purchase like a car or college. The point is to build the habit now, so it becomes automatic later. A habit that makes you financially free.

Breaking Free From the Rat Race

What is the rat race? Let me explain it simply.

The rat race is when you have to work to earn money to pay bills that require you to work to earn money to pay bills. Over and over. Round and round. Like a hamster on a wheel.

This is the life of most adults you know.

Wake up. Go to a job. Get a paycheck. Pay bills. The bills come again. Go back to work. Get another paycheck. Pay more bills. And it never ends.

Most people do this for 40 or 50 years. They work from age 22 to age 65, hoping they can finally rest when they retire.

But there is another way.

Breaking free from the rat race means your money works for you—instead of you working for money. It means you have investments earning interest while you sleep. It means you own a business that makes money even when you are not there. It means you get to decide how you spend your time.

Here is what financial freedom looks like: working 20 hours a week doing

something you love. Traveling when you want. Serving at your church without worrying about bills. Spending quality time with your family. Practicing for a triathlon. Taking a nap on a Tuesday. Going on vacation every other month without submitting a vacation request.

That is freedom. And you can have it by age 25 if you start now.

Here is how.

From age 15 to 20, you save $100 a month into Bucket 3: Saving.

That is $6,000 plus interest—let us call it $8,000.

From age 20 to 25, you get a real job and increase your savings. You put $500 a month into freedom. That is another $30,000 plus interest—let us call it $40,000.

By age 25, you have nearly $50,000 saved. That is enough to invest in a business. An online store. A coaching practice. A service company.

Avoid buying a job that ties you down to showing up 40+ hours a week after the initial setup. Choose a business that is not dependent on your physical presence more than 10hours each week. Choose a business that earns money even when you are not working.

You work your day job while building your side business. After a year or two, your side business earns $30,000, then $50,000, then $70,000. Once it replaces your day job income, you quit. You are free.

Note: I don't believe in retiring or not working at all. I don't see that in the Bible. Instead, I see a God who blessed each of us with talents and commanded us to multiply those talents. So, at every age, seek ways to bless and serve others by using the skills and passions God placed in you even if you choose to donate that money back and not collect an income.

Second Note: Not everyone is called to be an entrepreneur. And that is okay. If owning a business is not what God has placed in your heart, do not force it. Some people are called to build companies. Others are called to build within companies. Even more are called to build legacies inside businesses called Family. All are honorable. All can build wealth.

If working a full-time job is what you desire, then do it with everything you have. Pick a career you thoroughly enjoy. If working in the home is your passion, then do it joyfully. Show up every day with excellence. Colossians 3:23 says, "Whatever you do, do it heartily, as to the Lord and not to men." Your job is not a prison. It is a platform. You can build wealth right where you are—through the Four Buckets, through compound interest, through faithful stewardship over time. You do not need to start a business to break free from the rat race. You need to manage what you have with wisdom.

Some of the wealthiest people I know are teachers, nurses, and engineers who never owned a business. They simply saved consistently, invested early, and let time do the work.

If entrepreneurship is your calling, pursue it. If it is not, pursue excellence in your career or your home. Either way, do it as unto the Lord. He sees your work. And He rewards faithfulness.

You are free to work for pay, or not, and on your time.

You are 25 years old. You work when you want. You rest when you want. You serve when you want. You live. Free.

That is what breaking free from the rat race looks like.

Lies That Keep Young People Stuck

Before we end this chapter, I need to bust some myths. These are lies that society and culture sows into young people to believe about money. If you believe them, they will keep you stuck in the rat race forever.

Lie #1: You need debt to build credit.

False. You can live your entire life without a credit score. Millions of people do. You do not need a credit card. A debit card works for everything. A debit card has the same protection as a credit card with the same logo.

Lie #2: You need a high income to save.

False. Saving means putting money aside. That is all. I saved when I was making $50 a week. You can too.

Lie #3: Some people are just born good with money.

False. No one is born good with money. It is a skill you learn. If you practice, you get better. If you do not practice, you do not get better. You've learned many skills (tying your shoes, brushing your teeth, driving) and can learn another.

Lie #4: Budgeting is restrictive.

False. A budget is you telling your money where to go. You are the boss. You decide. That is freedom, not restriction.

Lie #5: Car payments are a way of life.

False. You do not need a car loan. Save up and pay cash. Buy a used car that runs well. Let someone else lose money on the new car smell.

Lie #6: You need student loans to go to college.

False. There are scholarships, grants, work-study programs, and community colleges. You can get an education without drowning in debt. You can save up for the expense and pay cash or pay as you go.

Lie #7: Renting is throwing away money.

False. There is a time to rent and a time to own. When you are young and figuring out life, renting gives you flexibility. Rent cheap. Keep expenses, including rent, to 60% of your income. Save the difference and buy when you are ready.

Lie #8: Living with your parents means you failed.

False. In most cultures outside America, families stay together. If your family is emotionally healthy and everyone is treated as an adult then living together saves everyone money. Split the bills. Keep more in your pocket. Invest the difference. Sow the seed into your future. That is wisdom, not failure.

Lie #9: You have to earn a massive income to build wealth.

False. Studies show that teachers—who do not earn huge salaries—are among the most common millionaires. Why? They put money aside consistently over time. Slow and steady wins the race.

Lie #10: Millionaires look like millionaires.

False. Read the book The Millionaire Next Door. Real millionaires drive used cars and live in modest homes. The people who look rich often have no money. They are maxing out credit cards. Do not try to keep up with the Joneses. The Joneses are broke.

A Word About Student Loans

I need to speak directly to emerging adults about the weight of student loan debt. You are soon to graduate high school and may consider secondary education, attending college or university.

Student loans have caused much harm to the financial landscape of many adults. Maybe you know someone who is carrying this weight for years—ten years, twenty-five years, longer. They talk about student loans like it is a life sentence. They make payments, but the balance barely moves. They do not even want to look at the number anymore.

And I want you to know there is a different path. Remember Lie # 6. You do not need a student loan to go to college.

I have my own history with student loans. I avoided them. I attended UCLA on a four-year scholarship. I got about ten thousand dollars in work study, free grant money, no loan. I confirmed this when I helped my son apply for FAFSA recently, there it was on my record. Most adults are still paying on their student loans while applying for student loans for their children.

Getting a scholarship was a blessing that I encourage others to actively seek as an option for college.

The other side of student loan story.

When I was dating my first husband, he needed help to finish paying for his undergraduate education. So I co-signed on his student loans. That was over twenty years ago. And those loans will continue to show up on my credit report until they are fully paid. I don't have to pay them, thankfully he makes the payments, but the reminder is there, the responsibility can legally shift to me.

Let that sink in. A decision I made in my early twenties—trying to help someone I loved—followed me for more than two decades. Is still following me. Cosigning is not a small thing. Your name on someone else's debt can make it your debt too.

I share this because I want you to know I understand. Student loans are heavy. They affect your credit, your options, your peace of mind. And when you do not have a plan, they feel impossible.

But here is what I have learned from helping others: the weight gets lighter when you name it.

I know a young professional who came to me with a significant amount of student loan debt. She had been carrying it for about ten years with no real plan. She just deferred the payments in hopes it would eventually go away.

It was not going away.

Together, we sat down and ran the numbers. We created a fifteen-year payoff plan—one that fit her life, one she could actually breathe in. Not a five-year plan that would suffocate her. A plan that matched her pace.

Then I showed her something that changed everything.

If she reduced her monthly payment by a few hundred dollars—which she was considering—it would add decades to her payoff and hundreds of thousands of dollars in interest. She had no idea. No one had ever shown her the math. Once she saw it, she made a different choice. She committed to the plan.

The transformation I see with student loan clients is not just financial. It is personal. They come in feeling like victims—like life happened to them, like they have no control. They leave feeling powerful. They have a plan. They have a number. They have an end date. They go from "I do not know where to start" to "I feel in control again."

That is what naming it does. That is what a plan does.

If you are carrying student loan debt, do not ignore it. Do not just hope it goes away. Sit down. Look at the numbers. Calculate when it will be paid off if you keep doing what you are doing. Then decide: is that acceptable?

Or do you want a different result?

You are a person of power. You signed for those loans—and you can sign off on a plan to eliminate them.

What About You?

If you are under the age of 25, you have something priceless: time. Do not waste it.

Here is what I want you to do. Ask yourself three questions:

First: Where do I want to be in 20 years? What kind of life do I want? How much freedom do I want? Be specific. Write it down.

Second: Where am I right now? Be honest. Do I have debt? Do I have savings? What is my mindset about money? What lies have I believed?

Third: Who will I follow? Who will I learn from? What books will I read? What community will I plant myself in that will help me grow?

Once you answer these questions, you can make a plan. You can start using the four buckets. You can automate your savings. You can watch your money make babies.

You were planted somewhere. But you do not have to stay there.

You can choose new soil. And the best time to plant is right now.

Reflection & Replanting

Take a moment to pause. Find a quiet place. Ask God to show you the path forward.

1. Where do you want to be financially in 20 years? Describe your ideal life.

____

____

____

2. Where are you right now? What is your current financial situation?

____

____

____

3. What money lies have you believed? Which ones will you stop believing today?

____

____

____

4. How will you divide your next paycheck using the four buckets?

____

____

____

5. What is one thing you will automate this week?

____

____

____

Chapter 2 Mantra

Say this out loud:

I can create wealth.
I have time on my side.
I will automate my future.
I will let my money make babies.
I will break free from the rat race.
I can create wealth.

You were planted somewhere.

But now you can choose new soil.

In the next chapter, we will learn how to walk this journey without walking alone.

Chapter 3 - Single Adults

You Don't Have to Walk Alone

If you are single, I need you to hear this: You are a whole person.

You are not half of something waiting to be completed. You are not broken because you do not have a ring on your finger. You are not less than because you live alone or eat dinner by yourself or file taxes as a single person.

You are whole. Right now. Just as you are.

And because you are whole, you can manage your money. You can build wealth. You can buy a house. You can plan for retirement. You can give generously. You can live a full and abundant life---without waiting for someone else to make it happen for you.

This chapter is for singles who accept that they are in a single season of life. It is for those who want to build a strong financial foundation before they ever walk down an aisle. It is also for those who have walked down an aisle, watched it crumble, and are now rebuilding on their own.

Either way, the message is the same: You do not need a spouse to be financially whole. But you do need to take responsibility for what God has placed in your hands.

The Condo I Never Chose

I got married, the first time, when I was 24 years old. I had been dating my husband since college. I thought I was ready.

When it came time to buy our first home---a condominium---I did not pull up a chair to the table. I did not ask questions. I did not look at listings. I did not tour properties. I deferred everything to him.

The first time I saw the condo was when we were signing the purchase papers.

I signed the paperwork. I packed and unpacked boxes. But I had no voice in the decision. The condo did not fit my character. It did not match who I was. It did not reflect my identity at all. But I said nothing.

That was my first lesson in what happens when you do not use your voice.

Early in the marriage, there was a season when my husband felt that he---as the man of the house---should manage the finances. So, I handed it over to him. But he did not know how. Checks started bouncing. Bills were missed. His way of handling money was getting us into trouble. So, he gave me back the responsibility of paying the bills.

When we divorced, the condo went into a short sale. We lost money. It sat on my credit report for years like a scar. A reminder that I had let someone else drive while I sat in the back seat with my eyes closed.

Two Years With My Parents

After my divorce, I moved back in with my parents. My son and I lived there for two years.

I want to be clear: this was my choice. I could have rented an apartment. I had enough money. But I chose community. I chose to be surrounded by people who loved me while I healed. I chose to let others carry some of the emotional weight while I got back on my feet.

But I did not move in as a child. I moved in as an adult.

I contributed to the household finances. Whatever I had been paying toward living expenses in my old home with my ex-husband, I gave to my parents. I was not a dependent. I was a contributing member of the household.

During those two years, I followed the Dave Ramsey baby steps with laser focus. I paid off all my debt. I saved a fully funded emergency fund.

Then I saved for six more months to build a down payment for a house.

My own house. That I would choose. That I would buy. By myself.

The House I Chose

Buying my first house was terrifying as a single parent.

I had never done it before. I had never walked through the process. I kept thinking: What if something goes wrong? What if I lose my job? What if I cannot make the payments? It is just me and my son.

But I trusted God. I trusted the plan. I trusted that I had prepared well---I had no debt, I had an emergency fund, I had savings. I had done the work.

So, I did it. I closed escrow. I got the keys. I walked into my house---the house I chose---and I cried.

That house proved something to me. It proved that I could follow a plan.

It proved that I could submit to a trusted system and it would work. It proved that I was a fully capable adult who could manage my own household.

I had a vision for the life I wanted my son to see. I wanted him to watch me make wise money decisions. I wanted him to grow up in a home where money was managed with intention. I wanted to raise him in the same community with the same beliefs, except about money. I did not want to raise him in the same financial soil I had been planted in.

So I chose new soil. For him and for me.

You Are a Steward

Before we go any further, I need to share something that changed how I see money.

The money in your bank account is not yours. It belongs to God. You are simply the steward---the manager---of it for a time.

Think of it like a teenager and their bedroom. The teenager did not buy the house. They did not pay for the furniture. But they are responsible for keeping the room clean. They make the bed. They put away their clothes. They take care of what has been entrusted to them.

That is what you are doing with money. God owns it. You manage it. And if you manage it well, it grows. It multiplies. It blesses you and others.

When you see yourself as a steward, everything changes. You stop asking, "How do I spend my money?" and start asking, "How does God want me to manage His money?"

That question will guide every financial decision you make.

The "I Can't Afford It Alone" Lie

Too many single people say, "I can't afford it alone." But what are they really saying?

Most of the time, they are living someone else's lifestyle. They saw it on social media. They saw their friends doing it. They see the home of a couple with two incomes. They want the car, the house, the vacations, the clothes---but none of it fits their actual income.

Here is the truth: most of those people are doing it on credit. They are in debt. They are stressed. They are acting rich, but they are broke.

Another truth: the single person compares themselves, in their twenties or thirties, to their parents in their fifties and sixties and expects to have the same result today that it took their parents 20-30 years to build.

You can afford what fits your budget. If you make $5,000 a month, you live a $5,000 a month lifestyle. If you make $10,000 a month, you live a $10,000 a month lifestyle. You do not borrow your way into someone else's life.

And if your income is low, you do two things: you keep your expenses even lower, and you work to increase your income over time. You do not wait for a spouse to rescue you. You rescue yourself.

You Can Save for Your Own Place

Maybe your goal is not living on less than you make. Maybe it is getting into a new place.

A new apartment. Your first home. A space that is completely your own---where you make the decisions, where you are not sharing a bathroom with a roommate, where you can come and go as you desire.

I have helped clients do exactly that. And I want you to know it is possible.

I worked with a young woman who was living with a family member. It was fine. It worked. But she wanted something different.

The problem was she did not know what she desired. So we sat down and did something simple but powerful: we gave her permission to dream.

What do you actually want? Where do you want to live this time next year? What matters to you?

As she answered those questions, something shifted. She realized she wanted her own apartment--- She wanted a space that was all her own---a place she could pick, a place that reflected who she was becoming.

Then we ran the numbers.

We looked at her income. We looked at her expenses. We named how much she was really spending on clothes, on shopping, on food. And we asked: what are you willing to adjust to get what you desire?

She made the adjustments. She created a six-month plan. And six months later, she moved into her very own apartment.

The transformation was beautiful. She went from "I don't need anything" to "I do not know how I can afford the thing I desire" to "I did it." Not "I can do it"---she already did it. Accomplished. Proud. Mature.

That is what happens when you stop guessing and start planning.

If you are single and dreaming of your own place, do not wait. Do not tell yourself it is impossible. Do not assume you need a spouse or a second income to make it happen.

Sit down. Dream. Then run the numbers. You might be closer than you think.

What about the single woman who says, "I'm waiting until I get married to buy a house"?

She is saying, "I am not valuable right now. I will be valuable when someone else chooses me."

That is a lie.

You are valuable now. Buy the house now. Save for it. Plan for it. Live your life fully right now. Do not hold your breath waiting for a ring.

Not everyone gets married. And even if you do, why delay your compound interest? Why delay your wealth? Why delay your joy?

God desires good things for His daughters and His sons---married or not.

What about the woman who says, "I need a husband to help me with finances"?

She is saying, "I cannot do this. I need someone to save me."

Would you say that to your ten-year-old self? Would you look at that little girl and say, "Only men have the intelligence to manage money"?

Of course not.

You have the ability to learn. You graduated school. You landed a job.

You can learn how to manage your personal finances. Read the books. Take the courses. Hire a coach. You are capable.

And men---this applies to you too. Do not delay buying property. Do not wait for a wife to start building wealth. Every year you wait is a year of compound interest you lose. Think about your future family. Set them up for success now.

Note: This is my general prescription without knowing your personal story. Wisdom may dictate you do something different in this season. Money is personal. Ask God what to do. Allow Him to be the final authority.

Partner vs. Dependent

If you do get married someday, you want to walk in as a partner---not a dependent.

What is the difference?

A partner walks beside their spouse. They pull up a chair to the table. They speak into decisions. They contribute---not just money, but ideas, questions, wisdom, and accountability. When their spouse is heading in the wrong direction, they speak up: "Wait. The map says we go this way."

A dependent walks behind their spouse. They stay quiet. They defer decisions. They do not ask questions. They do not learn. They assume their spouse knows everything---even when that spouse does not.

Here is the problem: no spouse is perfect. Everyone makes mistakes. If you enter marriage as a dependent, you suppress your voice to catch some of those mistakes. You just go along for the ride---even when the car is heading off a cliff.

And here is something else: studies show that the majority of wealth in the coming years will be managed by women. Why? Because of the three Ds---disease, divorce, and death.

When disease strikes a family, it often falls to the wife to manage the medical decisions, the insurance calls, and the finances---even while caring for a sick spouse or child. When a marriage ends through divorce, generally half the wealth goes to the wife. And it is still the case that about 65% of husbands die before their wives. The majority of the time, when a spouse dies, the wealth passes to the wife before it passes to the children.

Whether you planned for it or not, you will likely manage your family's finances at some point. You might as well learn now.

Being a partner does not mean you have to earn income. It means you contribute. You contribute knowledge. You contribute time. You contribute questions. You contribute support. You help find resources. You create a community around your family that supports wise money decisions.

That is what a partner looks like.

What to Build Before You Say "I Do"

If you are single and hope to be married someday, here is what I want you to build now:

1. Build your identity as a whole person.

Know who you are. Know what you believe. Know your values. If you do not feel whole, you will allow things in marriage that are not healthy. You will silence your voice. You will tolerate what you should not tolerate.

2. Build your financial literacy.

Read books. I recommend Know Yourself, Know Your Money by Rachel Cruze. It will help you understand your money history and how it shapes your decisions today. Also read The Total Money Makeover and The Automatic Millionaire. Listen to podcasts. Take courses. Never stop learning.

3. Build your wealth.

Get out of debt. Save an emergency fund. Start investing. Buy property if you can. The more wealth you build, the more you will attract people at your level---people with the same character of hard work, saving, generosity, and intentionality.

4. Build your standards.

Know what you will and will not accept. Make a list of must-haves and cannot-stands. Financial habits should be on that list. If you are debt-free and intentional with your finances, do not settle for someone who is comfortable in debt and doing nothing about it.

5. Build your relationship with God.

Ask Him about every purchase. Ask Him about every investment. Ask Him about every decision. He is your provider---married or single. He does not say, "I will supply all your needs if you have a spouse." His Word says that He "will supply all your needs according to His riches in glory by Christ Jesus." And His riches have no limit.

Red Flags to Watch For

When you start dating someone, pay attention to how they handle money.

Here are the red flags:

Red Flag #1: Dishonesty.

If there is no honesty, there is no relationship. If you catch them lying about how much something cost, how much debt they have, or how they spend their money---run. A small lie about money is a window into bigger lies later.

Red Flag #2: Comfort in a mess.

Having debt is not the red flag. Being comfortable in debt and doing nothing about it---that is the red flag. If you are working to get out of debt and they are not, you are heading in different directions. This will not take either of you very far.

Red Flag #3: No vision for the future.

If they are not talking about building wealth, leaving something for the next generation, or being generous---and those things matter to you---pay attention. Your present is not aligned. That will impact your future.

Red Flag #4: Opposite direction.

If their financial trajectory is going one way and yours is going another, you will be pulling against each other for the rest of your relationship. That would make for a hard marriage. Choose easy. Find someone going in the same direction.

But here is the key: you cannot spot these red flags if you do not know yourself first. You must be clear on who you are, what you believe, and what you will not accept. Then---when you see it in a date or potential marriage partner---you will know whether to stay or run.

God Provides for Singles

If you are a person of faith, I want you to hear this: God does not wait until you are married to provide for you.

Look at the Bible. Paul was never married. He worked with his own hands. He was content. God supplied all his needs.

Hagar was a single parent, alone in the desert with her son. God saw her. He provided a well of water at her deepest point of need.

The widow in 2 Kings had lost her husband to death and was soon to lose her two sons to debt, debtor's slavery. She had nothing---or so she thought. The prophet Elisha asked what she had. She had jars. God multiplied oil to fill every jar she had and those she borrowed. She sold the oil and paid her debts.

Over and over, the Bible shows God providing for the single, for the divorced, and for those who lost a spouse. We overlook these stories, but they are there.

2 Corinthians 9:8 says, "And God is able to make all grace abound to you, so that having all sufficiency in all things at all times, you may abound in every good work." It does not limit His grace to your spouse or your spouse's income. It says He is able to make His grace abound. It says you---not your spouse---may abound in every good work. His grace is abundant.

So, talk to God. Ask Him what He wants you to do with the money He has placed in your hands. Ask Him about every purchase, every investment, every decision. He is your provider. He is your partner. You are never truly alone.

What About You?

If you are single, I want you to ask yourself some hard questions:

Do I see myself as a whole person---or am I waiting for someone to complete me?

Am I managing my money with intention---or am I hoping someone else will figure it out for me later?

Am I living within my means---or am I borrowing someone else's lifestyle?

Am I building wealth now---or am I waiting for a ring to start?

Am I preparing to be a partner---or am I preparing to be a dependent?

Your answers matter. They will shape the kind of person you become. They will shape the kind of spouse you attract. They will shape the kind of legacy you leave.

You are not half of something. You are whole. And whole people can manage wealth.

Replanting Your Beliefs About Singleness

What beliefs were planted in you about being single?

Maybe you grew up believing that you are incomplete without a spouse---that marriage is what makes you whole. Maybe you inherited the belief that single people cannot build real wealth, buy homes, or plan for the future. Maybe you were taught that waiting for a partner is wiser than building alone.

These beliefs take root early. And when you find yourself single---whether by choice, by circumstance, or by season---those roots determine how you steward what God has given you.

If you grew up believing that you need a spouse to be financially whole, it is time to replant that belief. The new soil says: I am a complete person right now. I am capable of managing wealth. I do not need to be rescued.

If you inherited the belief that building wealth alone is pointless, dig it up.

Plant this instead: Every year I wait is a year of compound interest I lose. My future spouse---if one comes---will benefit from what I build today. My family of faith deserves a whole me today. Believers in my small group and church family are my family. They rely on me, and I rely on them. I have a family that depends on me. I am not waiting to create a family.

If you were taught that your value depends on your relationship status, uproot that lie.

The truth is: my identity is not in being married or single. My identity is in being a child of God. And He trusts me to steward what He has placed in my hands.

Examine the beliefs that were planted in you about singleness and money.

Keep the ones that produce good fruit. Uproot the ones that keep you waiting instead of building. And replant yourself in soil that will help you flourish---whether a wedding day ever comes or not.

Reflection & Replanting

Take a moment to pause. Find a quiet place. Ask God to reveal the truth about where you are.

1. Do you see yourself as a whole person? Why or why not?

____

____

____

2. What is your origin story with money? How has it shaped who you are today?

____

____

____

3. Are you living within your means---or borrowing someone else's lifestyle?

____

____

____

4. What financial red flags will you not tolerate in a future spouse?

____

____

____

5. What is one step you will take this week to build your financial future as a single person?

____

____

____

Chapter 3 Mantra

Say this out loud:

I am the manager of my wealth.
I am whole.
I do not need to be rescued.
God trusts me to manage what He has given me.
I can manage wealth.
You are not walking alone.

God is with you. And you are whole.

In the next chapter, we will learn how to move as one when two become one.

Chapter 4 - Married Couples

You Move as One or Not at All

Marriage is two people becoming one. Not just in body. Not just in heart. But in everything—including money.

When you said, "I do," you were not just joining your body. You were joining your bank accounts, your debts, your dreams, your fears, and your futures. From that day forward, there is no "my money" and "your money." There is only "our money."

This is hard for many couples to accept. It requires trust. It requires vulnerability. It requires honesty about things you may have never told another person.

But here is the truth: if you are not united in your finances, you are not truly united at all. You may live in the same house. You may sleep in the same bed. But if you are pulling in different directions with money, you are not moving forward together. You are stuck—or worse, you are drifting apart.

This chapter is about learning to move as one.

The Trinity Model

God gave us a picture of perfect unity: the Trinity.

God the Father, God the Son, and God the Holy Spirit are three different beings—yet they move and act as one.

Webster's dictionary defines marriage as: "The state of being united as spouses in a consensual and contractual relationship recognized by law." Notice that unity is built into the very definition—not just a Biblical concept, but a universally recognized one. They are never in conflict. They never work against each other. They never make decisions that the other would disagree with. They are perfectly united, as humans can be, in purpose, in character, and in direction. Even the law sees them as one.

Marriage is meant to be a reflection of that unity.

Imagine that you and your spouse are so united that you think and act as one—even when you are physically apart. Your spouse would not make a decision about time, energy, or money that you would disagree with. You would not make a decision about your body or relationships that your spouse would disagree with. Not because you are controlled by each other, but because you have talked so much, listened so deeply, and aligned so completely that you already know what the other would want. And you choose to be in harmony with them.

That is the Trinity model.

What does this look like with money? It looks like two people who have the same goals for the future—because they talked about it. They know how much they want to save. They know what they want to spend. They know what they are willing to sacrifice and what they are not. And because they are united, they can both make daily decisions that move them in the same direction. This doesn't mean one or both keep silent. The opposite. Both speak their truths. Both are free and safe to share their desires. Both feel welcomed and safe in the discussion. But once they pour all of that out on the table and make a decision—both honor the decision.

The husband does not buy a car without discussing it first. The wife does not rack up credit card debt in secret. Neither one makes financial decisions that would surprise or hurt the other—because they are one.

Two Horses, One Direction

The Bible says that two are better than one. But there is something even more powerful than that. Multiplication beats addition.

Consider Clydesdale horses. When they work alone, a single draft horse can pull about 5,000 pounds. You might think that two horses together could pull 10,000 pounds—just double the weight. But that is not what happens.

When two Clydesdale horses are teamed together and pulling in the same direction, they can pull 14,000 pounds or more. Their combined strength does not just add up—it multiplies. And here is the amazing part: the longer two horses train and work together, the more they get to know each other, the more weight they can pull. You'll often hear that two trained draft horses can pull up to 32,000 pounds together. That is a powerful picture of how alignment multiplies strength. Their power keeps increasing as their partnership deepens.

That is what happens when a husband and wife are united with their finances. Their wealth-building power is multiplied. Their ability to pay off debt, save for the future, and give generously is far greater together than it would be apart. And the longer they work together—the more they communicate, the more they trust—the stronger they become.

But here is the problem: if those two horses are pulling in opposite directions, they pull nothing. They dig their hooves into the mud and go nowhere. They may even tear the yoke apart.

That is what happens when a couple is not united with money. One spouse saves $100,000 for retirement while the other racks up $50,000 in credit card debt. What happens? The saver later uses half their savings to pay off the spender's debt. Now they have $50,000 together instead of $100,000. And if the spender's habits do not change, they will do it again—until there is nothing left.

If you are not pulling together, you are not pulling at all or worse, you are pulling apart.

You didn't get married to not move forward.

What I Learned From Two Marriages

I have been married twice. Both marriages taught me something about money and unity.

In my first marriage, my husband and I started with everything together. One joint account. One checkbook. Eventually I paid the bills and managed the budget. We tithed together. On the surface, it looked like unity.

But there was a problem. My husband did not pull up a chair to the table. He was not skilled with money and was not trying to get better. I handled everything alone. And over time, I started noticing things—charges on the account I did not recognize, money spent without a clear explanation. When I asked questions, the answers were not honest.

That was financial infidelity. And where there is financial infidelity, there is usually other infidelity too.

When we separated, we split our finances. We got back together for a time in an attempt to save the marriage. But we did not rejoin the finances. And once the money was separated, it was easy to walk away from the marriage. I learned something important: when there is no unity in finances, it is easy for there to be disunity in everything else.

In my second marriage, I tried to do things differently. On our honeymoon, we opened a joint account. I wanted unity from day one. He said he wanted unity too.

But my second husband never put his paycheck into that joint account. Every excuse was given. Every month, I waited. Every month, nothing changed.

We tried to have budget meetings, but he would not show up—or if he did, he could not stay focused on the conversation.

After a few months, it was clear: he was not being honest about his desire to be united. He wanted the pleasures of marriage without the partnership. That is not what marriage is.

One of the revealing arguments we had was about a family vacation. We agreed, in advance, to split the costs—I would pay for lodging, he would pay for activities and food. The vacation was fine. But then we got home and to the daily routines of life. Then I noticed that he did not pay his share of the household bills that month. When I asked why, he said I should have known he could not afford both the vacation and the bills.

But he never told me that in advance. We talked in advance. We budgeted in advance. He said he could afford it, in advance. It turns out "I can afford it" to him meant, "I can afford the fun but not the responsibility".

From both marriages, I learned this: unity requires honesty. Without honesty, there is no trust. Without trust, there is no unity. And without unity, there is no marriage—just two people living under the same roof, pulling in different directions.

Legally united, functionally divided.

Bound by covenant, living as individuals.

Married on paper, misaligned in practice.

Joined by law, separated by conviction.

Don't be this couple.

Naked With the Lights On

Why is it so hard for couples to talk about money?

Because money touches everything. It touches your past. It touches your trauma. It touches your family of origin. It touches your faith, your emotions, your fears, your dreams, your failures, and your shame.

Talking about money requires vulnerability. It requires you to be emotionally naked in front of another person—with the lights on.

Think about Adam and Eve in the garden before the fall. The Bible says they were naked and unashamed. They had nothing to hide. They could see each other fully—physically, emotionally, spiritually—and there was no fear, no judgment, no shame.

That is what marriage is supposed to be. Two people who can see each other fully and still love each other. Two people who can share their worst financial mistakes and not be judged. Two people who can admit their fears about money and be met with compassion instead of criticism.

Two people pulling in the same direction.

But most of us are not taught to be comfortable being naked—especially with money. We hide our debt. We hide our spending. We hide our fear that we do not know what we are doing. We are afraid that if our spouse sees the real numbers, they will think less of us.

A safe money conversation looks like this: both spouses are honest about their personalities, their skills, and their weaknesses.

One might be a saver. One might be a spender. Neither is wrong—they are just different.

The answer is: we will use both personalities to move toward our shared goals.

A safe money conversation also looks like this: both spouses share their dreams, their fears, their expectations, and their assumptions.

The answer is: we both give up something so together we get the most important thing.

What did you think marriage would look like financially?

What role did you think you would play?

What role did you think your spouse would play?

Your spouse may be failing a test they did not know they were taking—because you never told them what you expected.

If you do not feel safe talking about money with your spouse, that is a sign. Not a sign to exit the marriage, but a sign you need a marriage coach or counselor to help you build that safety. But do not ignore the sign. A marriage without financial honesty is a marriage built on sand.

Financial Infidelity vs. Financial Faithfulness

Fidelity means faithfulness. It means keeping your word. It means being trustworthy—not just today, but into the future. When you have faith in someone, you believe they will do what they said they would do, even when you are not watching.

Financial fidelity means your spouse can trust you with money. They can trust that you will spend according to what you agreed. They can trust that you will not open secret credit cards, hide purchases, or make major decisions without talking to them first.

Financial infidelity is the opposite. It is when you agree to do one thing and then do another. It is opening a credit card they do not know about. It is spending money on things—or people—you do not want them to see. It is not paying the mortgage payments without telling them, so the first clue they get is a foreclosure letter in the mail.

I have experienced financial infidelity in both of my marriages. In the first, it was charges I could not explain and answers that did not add up. In the second, it was a husband who filed taxes as single head of household—without telling me—after we agreed to file together as married filing jointly. The tax professional informed me that our filing was rejected because my husband had already filed and received his tax return through a different tax person. When I confronted my husband, he acted confused, as if he did not understand what year he filed taxes for.

Financial infidelity destroys trust. And without trust, there is no marriage.

Financial faithfulness looks different. It looks like transparency. It looks like telling your spouse before you make a big purchase—not after.

It looks like admitting when you are struggling, when the budget feels too tight, when you are tempted to use a credit card. It looks like treating your spouse as an adult whose opinion matters.

If you want to buy a car, you do not just show up with one in the driveway. You say, "I have been thinking about getting a new car. Can we talk about what that would look like for our family finances? What timeline works? What can we afford?" You include your spouse in big decisions—because you are one.

Both Must Be at the Table

It is dangerous for only one spouse to handle all the finances. Not because one person cannot do it alone—but because both people need to have a voice.

In most marriages, one spouse is the "nerd"—they love spreadsheets, budgets, and numbers. The other spouse is the "free spirit"—they would rather close their eyes and let someone else handle the numbers while they spend. This is not a gender thing. It can go either way.

It is fine for one spouse to manage the day-to-day details. But both spouses must be aware of the numbers. Both must have a voice in the decisions. Both must show up to the budget meeting. Both must agree.

I recommend a monthly budget meeting—at minimum. Sit down together and look at the accounts. How much came in? How much went out? What is coming up this month? Are there any concerns? Is this a financially tight month? Both spouses need to know so they can adjust their behavior accordingly.

If you are a spouse who says, "My significant other handles all the money—I do not even know our passwords," let me ask you this:

Would you be okay if you were a partner in a business, but the accountant never told you the financial outlook of your own company? Would you be okay if your child went to the doctor, but the doctor didn't share with you the diagnosis or the treatment plan?

Most adults would not accept being left in the dark in those situations.

So why accept it with your own money—your own livelihood—your own future?

Sometimes individuals opt out of finances so they can blame the other spouse when things go wrong. That is playing victim. You have the opportunity to engage. Use your voice. Pull up a chair. Ask for the passwords. This is your money too.

When my father passed away, my mother had to take over the finances. She was on all the accounts—my father was trustworthy—but she had let him handle everything. She did not know who to call, what was in each account, or what to do next. She figured it out because she is capable.

But it would have been easier if she had been at the table all along.

A Word for the Engaged

If you are engaged to be married, I have something important to say to you: do not wait until after the wedding to talk about money.

Money fights are still one of the top three reasons for divorce. Let that sink in. Couples who love each other deeply, who said vows before God and family, who dreamed of a lifetime together—they split up because they could not get on the same page about money.

You can avoid that. But you have to do the work before you say "I do."

Most couples getting married seek premarital counseling—and that is wise. But I highly recommend that you also get financial coaching. Not just a quick conversation about budgets. Real coaching that allows you to unpack your family of origin with money. To explore your relationship with money—your fears, your habits, your beliefs, your mistakes. To get everything out in the open before you join your lives together.

A good financial coach will help you and your future spouse:

- Understand how your childhood shaped your money beliefs

- Share your current financial situation—debts, savings, income—with complete honesty
- Set realistic expectations for how you will manage money together
- Create a safe environment where both of you can be completely honest
- Build a plan for how you will handle joint accounts, individual spending, giving, and saving

Do not go into marriage with surprises. Do not find out after the honeymoon that your spouse has $50,000 in debt they never mentioned. Do not assume you both have the same expectations when you have never actually talked about it, in detail.

Marriage is the joining of hearts, bodies, and finances. Prepare for all three. Get the counseling for your hearts. Have the conversations about physical intimacy. And get coaching for your finances.

The couples who do this work before the wedding are the couples who thrive after it. They go in with clear expectations. They go in with honesty. They go in as a team—already pulling in the same direction.

A System That Works

Here is a system that allows couples to be united while still being individuals:

Have one joint account for all shared expenses—rent or mortgage, utilities, groceries, insurance, savings, giving. All income goes into this account first. All bills come out of it. Both spouses can see it. Both spouses have access.

Then, agree on an amount for "fun money"—maybe $200 or $500 each per month, depending on your budget. Transfer that amount into separate personal accounts for each spouse.

This fun money is yours to spend however you want. If the wife wants to buy lipstick at Target, she does not have to ask permission. If the husband wants to buy a new tool at Home Depot, he does not have to explain himself. You are both adults. You both get to enjoy life.

But here is the key: you both agreed to this. It is not secret.

It is not hidden. It is part of the budget you created together. You are not doing your own thing—you are doing what you both decided, together.

This system gives you unity without losing your individuality. It gives you accountability without feeling like a child asking for allowance. It keeps you as a couple moving in the same direction while still letting you be an individual.

Your Individual Decisions Affect Your Family

The Bible is full of stories where one person's financial decision affected their entire family.

In Joshua 7, a man named Achan stole silver and gold that was supposed to be set apart for God. When his sin was discovered, his children were put to death along with him. His decision with money cost his children their lives.

In 2 Kings, there is a story of a widow whose husband had been a servant of the prophet Elisha. The husband died and left behind debt he could not pay. The creditors came to take the widow's two sons as slaves to pay off what was owed.

Think about that. The husband made a decision to go into debt. He did not plan for what would happen if he could not repay it. And when he died, his wife and children paid the price. The wife in 2 Kings might have said, "Let us find another way. Do not put me in a position where I could lose our children because of a decision you made today." But she was likely not at the table. She did not use her voice to request another option.

And then there is the story of Abigail and Nabal in 1 Samuel 25. Nabal was a wealthy man. During harvest season, David and his men had protected Nabal's shepherds and flocks. They worked hard and kept everything safe. When David sent messengers to ask for fair payment for their labor, Nabal refused. He insulted David. He acted as if David and his men deserved nothing.

Nabal's decision was so foolish, so unrighteous, that David strapped on his sword and prepared to wipe out all the men in Nabal's household—every single man. Because of one man's arrogance with money, other men connected to him were about to die.

But Abigail saved them.

The servants knew to go to the wife. They did not go back to Nabal—he was not listening. They went to Abigail because they trusted that she knew what was going on. They trusted that she could act. They knew she had been at the table.

And Abigail moved quickly. She knew where the resources were. She gathered bread, wine, sheep, grain, raisins, and figs—generous payment for the work David's men had done. She went to David herself, bowed before him, and apologized for her husband's foolishness. She pleaded with David to do the righteous thing and not take revenge.

David listened. He accepted her gift. He blessed her wisdom. And he turned his men around.

Abigail saved her husband's life. She saved the lives of ever man in her household. She did it by being wise, by knowing where the money was, by understanding what was happening, and by acting quickly when her husband would not.

That is what a quick-thinking, involved partner does. That is what happens when a wife pulls up a chair to the table. She does not act against her husband—she acts on behalf of him. She uses her wisdom and her access to resources to protect her family.

These stories carry a clear message: your financial decisions do not just affect you. They affect your spouse. They affect your children. They affect generations to come.

That is why both spouses need to be at the table. The widow was not at the table. She did not have a voice. And she almost paid the price. Abigail was at the table. She knew what was happening. She had access to the resources.

And when disaster came, she was able to act.

Pull up a chair. Speak into the decisions. Protect your family's future—together.

What About You?

If you are married, I want you to ask yourself some honest questions:

Are we truly united with our finances—or are we just living under the same roof?

Do I know what is in all of our accounts? Do I know our passwords?

Do I know our debts?

Do we have regular budget meetings—or do we avoid talking about money?

Have I been financially faithful—or have I hidden things from my spouse?

Do I feel safe being "naked with the lights on" about money—or do I hide parts or all of myself?

Am I pulling in the same direction as my spouse—or are we pulling apart?

Your answers matter. They will determine whether your marriage moves forward together—or stays stuck in the mud.

Two are better than one. But only if they are moving in the same direction.

Replanting Your Beliefs About Marriage and Money

What beliefs were planted in you about money in marriage?

Maybe you grew up believing that one spouse should handle all the finances while the other stays uninvolved. Maybe you inherited the belief that separate accounts protect you—that keeping your money apart keeps you safe. Maybe you were taught that fighting about money is normal, unavoidable, even expected.

These beliefs take root early. And when you enter marriage, those roots determine whether you pull together or pull apart.

If you grew up believing that only one spouse needs to understand the finances, it is time to replant that belief. The new soil says: both partners must be at the table. Both must have access. Both must have a choice and a voice. Marriage is partnership, not delegation.

If you inherited the belief that separate finances protect you, dig it up. Plant this instead: unity requires vulnerability. If I am not willing to join my finances, I am not fully joining my life. Trust is built through transparency, not through walls.

If you were taught that money fights are inevitable, uproot that lie. The truth is: couples who communicate about money—who have regular budget meetings, who share their dreams and fears, who agree before they spend—do not have to fight. Conflict comes from secrecy, surprise, and misalignment.

Unity brings peace.

Examine the beliefs that were planted in you about marriage and money.

Keep the ones that draw you closer to your spouse. Uproot the ones that create division. And replant yourself in soil where two can truly become one.

Reflection & Replanting

1. On a scale of 1-10, how united are you and your spouse with finances? Why did you choose that number?

____

____

____

2. What expectations did you bring into marriage about money that you have never spoken out loud?

____

____

____

3. Is there anything about your finances that you have hidden from your spouse? What would it take to be honest?

____

____

____

4. When was the last time you had a budget meeting with your spouse? When will the next one be?

____

____

____

5. What is one thing you can do this week to move toward greater financial unity?

____

____

____

Chapter 4 Mantra

Say this out loud with your spouse:

We can manage wealth.
We are one.
We pull in the same direction.
We are honest with each other.
Together, we do more with wealth.

Two horses pulling together can move mountains.

Two spouses united can build generational wealth.

In the next chapter, we will learn how to teach the next generation not to eat the seed.

Chapter 5 - Parents

You Teach What You Want to Grow

The greatest financial gift you can give your children is not money. It is wisdom.

You can leave your children an inheritance, but if they do not know how to manage it, they will lose it. You can pay for their college, but if they do not understand the value of work, they will waste the opportunity. You can give them everything they want, but if they do not learn to steward what they have, they will always feel like they do not have enough.

This chapter is about planting seeds in your children---seeds of wisdom, character, and financial responsibility---that will bear fruit for generations.

Because what you teach is what will grow.

The Oak Tree

I love this picture: imagine sitting under a beautiful oak tree on a hot summer day. The branches spread wide above you. The leaves block the harsh sun. You are shaded from the heat, protected from the storm, sheltered from the trials beating down around you.

But here is the thing---you did not plant that tree.

Someone else planted it. Someone else watered it. Someone else protected it when it was just a tiny seedling. And now, years later, you get to enjoy the shade.

That is how I feel about my life. My parents planted a seed when we immigrated to this country. They worked hard. They sacrificed. They poured blood, sweat, and tears into building a life for their children. And now I get to sit under the shade of the tree they planted.

Some people call this being "born on third base." The child did not hit the ball. They did not run to first or second. They simply showed up on third base---and all they have to do is run home to score. But sometimes children think they hit the ball themselves. They do not realize the sacrifice that got them to third base.

But I want to give you an admonition here. The Scriptures tell a story about three stewards in Matthew 25. A master left his servants with talents---one received five, another three, and another received one. Each was expected to be fruitful and multiply what they had been given.

The one with five talents multiplied them and gained five more. The one with three multiplied them and gained three more. But the one with just one talent tucked it away, buried it in the ground, and added nothing to it. When the master returned, he was not pleased with the servant who buried his talent.

Here is my caution: Be careful when looking at whether you were born on first, second, or third base. You may think you were only born with one talent because you have not opened your eyes to see all the blessings already in your account. Your talents may not be financial---but character, relationships, physical strength, and mental endurance are all talents you were born with. Comparison robs you of seeing the wealth you already have.

I want to remind you: you have wealth. You have a wealth of experience, ability, and blessing that God has already given you. So do your children. He wants you, and them, to multiply it---not bury it.

As a parent, your job is to plant trees your children will sit under. Not by giving them stuff---but by giving them character. Hard work. Generosity. Wisdom. Faith. These are the seeds that grow into shade for the next generation.

What kind of tree are you planting?

Start When They Can Count

When should you start teaching your children about money? As soon as they can count.

Use money to teach them numbers. One dollar. Two dollars. Three dollars. Let them hold the coins. Let them hold the bills. Make it real.

From the time my son could count, I involved him in counting change at the grocery store. We used an envelope system while I was getting out of debt. He knew what the budget was for that shopping trip. And I made it a game---if we came in under budget, he could add a small item to the cart.

This taught him several things at once: money is limited, choices have to be made, and staying under budget is a win.

As he got older, the conversations grew with him. We talked about back-to-school shopping budgets. We talked about what college would cost and how we would pay for it; his dad's part, his mom's part, and his part. We talked about job losses and promotions---age-appropriately---so he understood what was happening in our household without feeling anxious.

I never wanted him to see stress on my face and not understand what was causing it. So when I was laid off, I told him: "This is what happened. But this is what Mom already did. I have money saved. You are not going to be negatively impacted. You can still do your activities." I wanted money conversations to be open and safe in our home. Not scary. Not secret. A good normal.

The Bible says in Deuteronomy to teach your children when you are at home, when you are on the road, when you are going to bed, and when you are getting up. Basically, teach them all the time and everywhere. That means money lessons happen in the car on the way to school. At the grocery store. At the dinner table. In the moments of everyday life.

Start when they can count. And never stop.

The First Job Interview

When my son was five years old, he interviewed for his first job.

I believe children should work---not be handed money just for existing. I still believe this. It is not enforcing an earning mentality but establishing a character of hard work. There is a balance.

So, at five years old, my son put on a little suit. I sat him down and asked him interview questions---age-appropriate, of course. What job do you want? Why do you think you would be good at it? Are you ready to do this every week?

He chose to empty the trash. We agreed on the payment. I hired him. And he did the job.

Every birthday after that, he accepted a new responsibility. After emptying the trash came folding and putting away his laundry. Then cleaning the bathroom. By the time he was ten, he had five chores he was responsible for in the house.

This was not about cheap labor. It was about building character. I wanted him to feel his own strength. I wanted him to know he could contribute. I wanted him to understand what it takes to contribute in a household---so that when he grows up, he will not carry a dependent mentality into his own home.

Should children get an allowance? I believe it should be tied to work. Not because I want to be harsh---but because I want to prepare them for real life.

In the real world, the adult world, most people do not get a trophy just for showing up. You do not get paid for existing. You earn it.

When children work for their money, they value it differently. They think twice before spending it. They feel the weight of what it took to earn it. And they grow in confidence, knowing they can actually do hard things.

Four Things to Do With Money

When my son was young, I gave him a piggy bank with three compartments.

It taught him that there are different things you do with money---not just spend it.

I taught him four things to do with money: Earn it. This category later turns into Pay Bills. Give it. Save it. Spend it.

This simple system taught my son that money has purpose. It is not just for buying things. It is for giving, for building security, and for enjoying life---in that order.

Over the years, he saved for things he wanted. A Nintendo DS. An Xbox---he paid for half of each himself when he was about ten and twelve years old. Then his car.

I told him: "When it is time to buy a car, whatever you have saved, I will match it." So, he saved.

And when he turned sixteen, we went car shopping together, with his savings and my match for a gently used car. A starter car he could grow from.

We searched for cars in full faith that he would pass his driving test in the coming weeks. He had skin in the car buying game. It was his car---not a gift he had done nothing to earn. But here is the part I am most proud of: my son got to watch me pay cash for his car. I left him at the car dealership, went to get the money, and came back with cold, hard cash. No lease. No loan. No monthly payments---ever. We drove off the lot that day owning the car outright.

He also got to experience the salesman asking whose car it was. And he got to tell them that he had saved up for it. That he had worked, collected birthday money, and put money aside. That it was his car. That was a beautiful moment---watching my son stand tall and say, "I earned this."

That experience planted a seed. He saw with his own eyes that you do not have to go into debt to buy a car. You can save. You can pay cash. You can drive away free.

More Is Caught Than Taught

Rachel Cruze says it well: "More is caught than taught."

Your children are watching you. They see how you react when money is tight. They see whether you panic or stay calm. They see whether you pull out a credit card or pay with cash. They see whether you give generously or reluctantly. They see whether you buy impulsively or wait and save.

You can tell your children to trust God with their finances. But if they see you anxious and panicked every time a bill comes, they will not believe your words. They will believe your actions.

This is why modeling matters. Your children will do what you do---not what you say.

But here is the other side: talking matters too. Because children do not always understand what they are seeing.

To a young child, a credit card and a debit card look the same. They might see you swipe a card and think, "Mom said we do not use credit cards, but she just used one." They do not know the difference unless you explain it.

So, talk about what you are doing. "This is a debit card. The money comes straight out of my bank account. A credit card is different---it is borrowing someone else's money then paying it back, and often, with interest."

Children see things from a different angle. They are looking from the floor, from the backseat, from a limited perspective. Your words provide context for what they are seeing. Without that context, they will fill in the blanks themselves---and they might get it wrong.

Model good habits. And talk about what you are doing. Both are necessary.

Make Giving Visible

One thing my parents did well was make giving visible.

When we went to church, they gave each of us a dollar to put in the offering. We got to experience what it felt like to give. We saw them put their own money in the bucket. We watched generosity in action---not just heard about it.

This is one area where I struggled with my own parenting. I automated my tithing. The money came out of my account automatically every month. It was efficient. It was consistent. But it was invisible.

My son rarely saw me give. He heard me talk about tithing, but he did not see the money leave my hand and go into the church bucket. And I believe that made it harder for him to connect with giving as something real.

Automation is great for building wealth. But when it comes to teaching your children, some things need to be visible. They need to see the sacrifice. They need to see the envelope. They need to see the check being written or the cash being handed over.

If you want your children to have a heart for giving---not just a habit of giving---let them see you do it. Let them hold the money. Let them put it in the bucket themselves. Make it real.

Over the years, I have increased my giving beyond ten percent. Every year, I raise it---sometimes by half a percent, sometimes by a full percent. I do this because God has been generous to me, and I want to reflect that generosity back. I have these conversations with my son, so he understands why I give, not out of guilt, but out of gratitude.

Tithing is not just a rule. It is a heart posture. And heart postures are caught by watching---not just taught by telling.

Turn Off the TV

Here is something I did that made a bigger difference than I expected: I turned off the television.

In my home growing up, the TV felt like it was always on. Even when we were watching neutral or good things---news, Wheel of Fortune, Christian programs---there were still advertisements. And ads have one job: to make you feel like you are missing something. To make you want what you do not have. To keep you chasing the next thing.

That is the "keeping up with the Joneses" mentality. And it starts young.

In my adult home with my son, the TV is rarely on. I have a smart TV, so on the rare occasion the tv is on, I choose to watch things without commercials. This meant my son was not constantly bombarded with messages telling him he needed the latest toy, the newest gadget, the coolest shoes.

It is hard to be content when a hundred voices a day are telling you that you are not enough without their product. By turning off those voices, I gave my son space to be grateful for what he had instead of wanting to fill a void.

This is a small thing. But small things add up. Guard what comes into your home. Guard what voices your children hear. Because those voices shape what they believe about money, about success, and about themselves.

Expose Them to Good Wealth

Growing up, I saw wealthy people in the news being criticized. I saw family friends who got rich through dishonest means---and then lost everything when they got caught. Based on those experiences, I became afraid of wealth. The message I absorbed was: wealthy people are bad. Wealth disappears. Do not aim too high.

I was determined to do something different with my son and chose to start from an early age. I wanted him to see wealth that was good.

Wealth that was earned honestly. Wealth that was sustained over time. Wealth held by people with great character who loved God and loved others.

So, I made sure he was exposed to it. We have friends who are wealthy---not flashy or arrogant, just comfortable and generous. My son has been in their homes. He has played in their backyards. He has seen that they are kind, humble, and hardworking. They did not get rich by cheating. They built wealth over decades by being responsible and trusting God.

For his entire seventeen years, my son has watched these families grow in wealth---steadily, sustainably. He has seen that wealth does not have to disappear. It can be built and kept and passed down. This matters because children need to see what is possible. If the only wealthy people they see are corporate villains, criminals in the news, athletes and musicians, they will believe wealth is bad or only for a select few. But if they see real people in various industries, giftings, and ages---people they know and love---living generously and building wealth with integrity, they will believe it is possible for them too.

Show your children what good wealth looks like. Let them touch it. Let them see it up close. Plant those seeds.

The Legacy You Leave

What legacy do you want to leave your children?

I want my son to know that I loved God and loved people. I want him to see that I did everything in my power to serve God and serve others---including him---without neglecting myself. I want him to understand that I valued myself because God values me. That I moved with excellence because my God is excellent. That I showed mercy because God has shown me so much mercy.

I want my son to see that I reflected God's character---even when I messed up. That I kept aiming for it. And one of God's characteristics is that He is a provider. A God of abundance. A protector.

I want my son to see that I provided for my household. That I had wealth---not to show off, but to protect my family from the storms of life. That I worked hard and planned ahead so that when trouble came, we were ready.

And I want him to do the same. To work hard. To provide for his household. To reflect the character of God as a provider and protector. To build wealth that serves his family and blesses others.

The seeds you plant in your children are not just about money. They are about character. Hard work. Generosity. Faith. Excellence. Kindness. Honesty. Vulnerability. These are the seeds that grow into shade for the next generation.

My father taught me that love is sacrificial. By sacrificing some of my pleasures---not all, but some---and putting that money aside for my son's future, I am planting a tree he will sit under one day. A tree of education without debt. A tree of opportunity. A tree of wisdom.

What tree are you planting for your children?

What About You?

If you are a parent, I want you to ask yourself some honest questions:

Are money conversations safe in my home---or are they filled with stress and secrecy?

Am I teaching my children to work for money---or just handing it to them?

Do my children see me give---or is my generosity invisible to them?

What voices am I allowing into my home? Are they building contentment or creating craving?

Have I exposed my children to good wealth?

What character am I modeling? What will my children catch from watching me?

Your answers matter. They will shape what your children believe about money, about work, about generosity, and about God.

You are planting seeds every day. Make sure they are seeds you want to grow.

Reflection & Replanting

1. What money lessons did you learn from your parents? What do you want to repeat? What do you want to change?

____

____

____

2. How can you make money conversations safer and more normal in your home?

____

____

____

3. What chores or responsibilities could your children take on to learn the value of work?

____

____

____

4. How can you make your giving more visible to your children?

____

____

____

5. What is one seed of character or wisdom you want to plant in your children this week?

____

____

____

Chapter 5 Mantra

Say this out loud:

I can use wealth for good.
I am planting seeds of wisdom in my children.
I model what I want them to become.
I am building a legacy that will outlast me.
My children will sit under the shade of the tree I plant today.

The greatest inheritance is not money. It is wisdom.

Plant seeds today that will bear fruit for generations.

In the next chapter, we will learn how to steward wealth when life takes an unexpected turn.

Chapter 6 - Disease Divorce & Death

When the Garden Burns Down

Sometimes the garden you planted burns to the ground.

You did your best. You planted seeds. You watered them. You waited for the harvest. And then fire came—whether through one of the three D's, disease, divorce or death—and everything you built is gone.

If that is where you are right now, I want you to know something: I see you. We serve a God who sees us. He wants you to feel his compassion in this season. Receive the warmth of that loving embrace first and foremost.

Then, look up. Open your eyes as Hagar did and see the well of water.

Provision is already available.

You can replant. The soil is still good. The sun still shines. And God is still faithful.

This chapter is for those who have walked through disease, divorce, or death—and must now rebuild their financial life.

Maybe you lost a spouse. Maybe you lost years of income to illness. Maybe you lost your savings to medical bills. Whatever the fire looked like, you are here now. And you can rebuild.

It is not easy. But it is possible. And you can come out of this season stronger, wiser, and more whole than before.

When Disease Drains the Garden

Not every fire comes from divorce or death. Sometimes the fire is disease.

Studies show that medical bills are the leading cause of bankruptcy in the United States. More than half of all bankruptcy filings are connected to medical expenses or illness-related income loss. And this is not just happening to the uninsured. Families with good jobs and good insurance are losing a significant portion of their wealth because one diagnosis changed their lives overnight.

I have watched disease burn down gardens in my own family.

When I was in my first year at UCLA, my mother was diagnosed with breast cancer. She was running her own nursing practice at the time—building something of her own. The diagnosis did not just affect her body. It affected her business. It affected her ability to work. It affected how much she could contribute to the family while she was fighting for her life.

Our African community and our church family rallied around her. They showed up. They helped carry the weight. And by God's grace, she survived. She beat the cancer.

Then, years later, she was diagnosed again.

And she beat it... again.

My mother is a fighter. But disease does not ask permission. It does not wait until your finances are in order. It does not care how hard you have worked or how carefully you have planned. It simply comes.

Then... it came for my sister.

She had just given birth to her third child when she detected breast cancer. She was married. She had two other children at home. And now she had to fight for her life while recovering from childbirth.

She was out of work for an extended period—months of treatment, months of recovery. Thankfully, her husband was also working. He took such great care of my sister, and still does. But her income was impacted. Her contribution to the household finances was impacted. And the bills kept coming.

The family rallied around her the way we had rallied around my mother. We helped with the children—picking them up from school, making sure they did not miss anything while their mother was in treatment. We carried what we could carry.

She beat it. By God's grace, my sister is still here.

But the financial impact was real. The time lost was real. The strain on the family was real.

Disease can run in families. It struck my mother twice. It struck my sister. And I have had to face my own scares—staying on top of screenings, doing the tests, taking precautions. I do my part to be aware. But I cannot predict the future. None of us can.

That is why preparation matters.

The best time to prepare for disease is when you are healthy. The best time to build your emergency fund is before the emergency. The best time to make sure you have adequate insurance is before the diagnosis, before the car accident, and before the financial provider passes away.

If you never need your emergency fund, that is amazing. If you never have to dip into your savings for a medical crisis, praise God. But life happens. Change happens. Disease happens. And when it does, you want to have something to fall back on.

We cannot predict the future. Only God can. But we can prepare. We can put money aside for whatever may come—whether it is an accident, an illness, a death, or a divorce. We can do our part and trust God with the rest.

If you are walking through disease right now—whether your own or a loved one's—I see you. God sees you. The fire is real. The pain is real. But the soil is still good. And you can rebuild.

What I Learned From Two Divorces

Both my divorces taught me something different about money, identity, and healing.

After my first divorce, I had debt—some of which I got into because I did not speak up for myself. I also had a child to raise, and I made the decision to take on one hundred percent of the daily household expenses and responsibilities. The father paid child support, but I never asked him for anything beyond that. I simply carried any and all additional weight.

Getting out of debt was one of the hardest financial decisions I made. For two years, I did not do anything fun. I love traveling. I love the theater. I enjoy getting my hair done. But during that season, I gave all of that up. I found other ways. I sacrificed. I also made the decision to set money aside for my son's college—every month, for years—so that he could graduate without debt by following an agreed plan. That meant I did not take all the vacations I wanted. I did not buy all the things I wanted. I did not drive the cars I would have liked to drive. I planted seeds instead for my son's future.

It took about two years to stabilize financially after my first divorce. I followed the Dave Ramsey system. I did my debt-free scream with my son—not on a stage, but in our living room. I AM DEBT FREE!!!

My second divorce was different. Even though I was married, I was managing money alone. My husband never allowed us to unite our finances. I wanted a partner to do the budget with—not to hand over control, but to share the responsibility. That never happened. When that marriage ended, there was no financial loss. All the financial weight had been on my shoulders during the marriage. After the divorce, I simply updated my spreadsheets and moved on. The stabilization was immediate—because we had never truly been united.

But I still had to grieve. Not the loss of money—the loss of my expectation. The loss of the partnership I had hoped for. The loss of the intimacy of sharing life with someone I trusted.

From both marriages, I learned this: you can survive financial loss. You can rebuild. And sometimes, the fire that burns down your garden is the very thing that clears the ground for something better.

Identity After Loss

Divorce affects more than your bank account. It affects your identity.

After my first divorce, I lost the title of "Mrs." For some people, that identity is everything. But I learned something important: my identity is not in my marital status. It is not in being a wife. It is not even in being a mother—as much as I love being Mom.

My identity is in being a child of the one true King. That is the only identity that does not change. Money changes. People change. Homes change. Marital status changes. But God does not change. And when I attached my identity to Him alone, I found peace.

There was shame after my first divorce—especially because I was in a community where no one got divorced. When I asked my parents who I could talk to about what I was going through, at that time they could not think of a single person. It felt lonely.

But God walked me through it. I came out without depression, without addiction, without unhealthy relationships. I came out whole—actually, better than whole. I came out with a greater sense of who I am, what God made me to do, and the fact that I deserve my healthy boundaries to be respected.

My first divorce was one of the best things that ever happened to me. Not because divorce is good—but because God used it to strip away everything that was not Him, so I could finally see that all I really need is Him.

After my second divorce, I came out even more refined. That relationship caused me to question my thoughts, my decisions, my sanity. But when I came out the other side, I was more solid, more golden, more certain of my identity. I know that I make good decisions. I know that I am trustworthy with anything, including money. I know that I use wealth for good.

If you are going through divorce right now, know this: people will judge you no matter what. They will judge you if you stay in a marriage.

They will judge you if you leave. So, stop living for their approval. Marriage is a covenant between people and a covenant with God. He sees the impact of a broken covenant. He alone is the righteous judge. Live for God's approval. And trust that He can bring beauty from ashes.

Trust that the same God who saw Hagar, sees you.

Face Your Front

There is a Nigerian saying: "Face your front."

In Nigerian culture, this phrase means to mind your own business, stay focused on what you are doing, and avoid distractions from others. It encourages you to look ahead and be present and attentive to your own actions and responsibilities.

I love this saying because it applies perfectly to life after divorce or loss. The windshield is much bigger than the rearview mirror for a reason. You are meant to look forward, not backward.

If you keep staring at the fact that your marriage failed, you are looking in the rearview mirror.

But if you look through the windshield, you will see something different: an opportunity. An opportunity to develop yourself financially. An opportunity to make wise decisions. An opportunity to start fresh.

What do you say to someone who feels like they failed financially because their marriage ended?

I would say this: replace the word "failure" with "experiment."

You tried something. You made the best decision you could with the information you had at the time. Show yourself grace. And then move forward.

This is a new day. The sun is still shining. Life goes on. Just because you do not have a spouse does not mean your life is over. God is still good—He did not change. Only your circumstances have changed. And circumstances always change.

So, face your front. Move forward. Keep going in a forward direction.

This is the day that the Lord has made. Choose to rejoice and be glad in it.

Do Not Go Alone

One of the biggest mistakes people make after divorce is trying to do everything alone.

The Bible says that two are better than one. They keep each other warm.

After my first divorce, I had to admit that—and I chose to accept my parents' offer to move into their home.

Honestly, I believe that saved me. It saved me heartache, emotional pain, depression, and unnecessary trauma. My parents were not therapists. They did not have all the answers. But their presence was healing in a way that is hard to put into words. Their presence protected me from bad decisions—including bad financial decisions.

Find a community where you are loved. It does not have to be people who have been through divorce—just people who care about you and will be there for you. Often, they are family.

Then find a community of people who have experienced divorce and can help you navigate it in a healthy way. I have led a small group at my church, the South Bay Campus of Saddleback Church, for almost ten years—divorced, widowed, and never married mothers. We share the grief, the hurts, the unfulfilled expectations. We talk about finances, careers, raising children alone. That community has been life-giving.

I also got professional help. I went to therapy—not because I was falling apart, but because I wanted preventative medicine. I was not depressed, but I did not want to become depressed. I was not bitter, but I did not want to become bitter. A therapist helped me navigate life on a consistent basis so I could continue to heal. Opening up to a professional gave me a safe space to process my pain without overwhelming the people I loved most.

Getting professional help does not mean you are unhealthy. It shows you are healthy enough to ask for help. And that helps you stay healthy. Do not go through this alone.

Practical Steps After Divorce

If you are going through or have recently been through a divorce, here are practical steps to protect yourself financially:

- Run your credit report.
- Close joint bank accounts.
- Review all credit cards and debts.
- Change beneficiaries.
- Get life insurance if you have children.
- Review housing and car titles.
- Update utilities and bills.
- Create a new budget.
- Change your name if desired.

Fight for what you need

Too often divorcees feel like they should not ask for what is theirs. Identify what is yours—what you brought into the marriage—and make sure you leave as whole as possible.

At the same time, be willing to let go. Some people drag out divorce for years because they want to hold on to a house or a car. Your mental health is worth more than any asset. You can buy another house. You can earn more money. Buy another car. But you cannot get back the years you spent fighting over things that do not matter.

Here is something harder to admit: some people drag out a divorce not because of assets, but because it keeps them connected to their former spouse. It is a way to stay in touch, to stay relevant, to maintain some thread of association. This can be subconscious—you may not even realize you are doing it. But if you find yourself prolonging the legal battle beyond what is necessary, ask yourself honestly: am I holding on to the process because I am not ready to let go of the person?

Get emotionally healthy. Work with a therapist or counselor if needed. Do the inner work so you are not inadvertently dragging out your divorce just to maintain a connection that has already ended. It is okay to let go. Letting go of the legal battle is part of letting go of the person.

Let it go. Your peace is worth it.

If Your Spouse Handled All the Money

If your spouse handled all the finances and now you are on your own, take it slowly. Show yourself grace. Do not judge yourself for what you did not know.

If you made the decision to take a backseat, own it. You are not a victim. You made a choice—and now you can make a different choice. Say to yourself: "I am no longer taking a backseat with my finances. It is my responsibility now. I will pull up a chair at the table."

Lean into how you learn. If you learn by watching, find YouTube videos.

If you learn by doing, take a class. Create time to learn what you did not learn before—but do not overwhelm yourself. Focus on the most important thing first.

In month one, focus on the basics: open a bank account in your name, make sure your income goes into it, and set up payments for your bills—utilities, car insurance, medical insurance, cell phone. That is a huge win.

In month two, start building a budget. Write down all your income and expenses. Gather passwords. Create a system.

Give yourself three months to try a system and tweak it. You might start with a spreadsheet and realize you hate it. That is fine—try something else. Find what works for you.

Use a proven system—something millions of people have used successfully.

Do not reinvent the wheel. Submit to a system and follow it.

And remember the Four Buckets. You can give. You can earn and pay bills. You can save. You can have fun. Put money aside to breathe and enjoy life. Just because you are single does not mean life is over. There is much opportunity ahead.

Healthy Boundaries With Your Ex

One of the biggest challenges I see with couples after divorce is difficulty letting go.

When a spouse dies, there is a finality to it. But when a marriage ends through divorce, that person is still alive. There is a temptation to still try to control them, speak into their life, or have expectations of them.

But the marriage is dead. Once the divorce is final; bury it.

Grieve it and treat it as the dead thing it is.

You would not keep opening a casket if the person were physically dead.

Do not keep reopening the tomb of your dead marriage.

If there are children involved, the only conversations you need to have with your ex are about the children—co-parenting, pickup times, vacations, logistics. That is it.

There are rare situations where the ex-spouses remain friends with healthy boundaries. If that is not your story, bury the marriage and walk away.

Safeguard your heart. Safeguard your finances.

But just as important—respect the boundaries of the other person. You no longer get to speak into their money, their time, their energy, or their relationships.

Be careful to respect the boundaries of the dead.

One decision I made after my first divorce was to make sure child support was automatic. It was decided during the divorce and visitation proceedings. I fought then to ensure everything flowed through the legal system. And we never had to fight about it again. Not one argument.

That protected both of us—and it protected my son from seeing his parents fight about money.

I also chose to not be bitter. One way I avoided bitterness was by making sure his father contributed financially. That way, when my son grows up, he can say his dad was physically present in his life and financially involved. That mattered to me, so I used my voice to advocate for my mental peace.

For the Widows and Widowers

If you have lost a spouse to death, my heart goes out to you. This is one of the hardest things a person can walk through.

My mother became a widow when my father passed away. She had retired from her nursing career, and my father had officially retired but was still working as a substitute teacher. He worked up until the short illness that led to his death. When he died, my mother was left with debt—including a mortgage—and became solely responsible for paying it. Thankfully, my father had some retirement benefits that helped sustain her.

But here is something I must share honestly: my father believed life insurance was important. Yet he and my mother chose to let one of their life insurance policies lapse a year and a half before he passed away. The premiums felt heavy at the time, and they could not see the future.

Because of that decision, my mother did not receive all his life insurance benefits. She could have paid off the mortgage and the credit card debt right away. Instead, she is managing it month by month. I share this not to shame my parents, but to urge you: do not let your life insurance lapse. You do not know what tomorrow holds. The cost of the premium is nothing compared to the burden you could leave behind.

This is for those with a spouse and dependent children; those relying on your income and financial provision.

Do Not Make Big Decisions While Grieving

If you have just lost a spouse, here is my strongest advice: do not make any big financial decisions in the first year.

Grief is deceptive. From day to day, you may feel fine—and then a wave crashes over you unexpectedly. You may feel angry, sad, depressed, or numb. These emotions affect your judgment, even when you do not realize it.

Do not sell the house. Do not relocate. Do not make major purchases. Do not invest a large inheritance. Just pay for the things that need to be paid—do the minimum—and let yourself grieve.

Let other people help. People you trust who can think more clearly. Let them lift some of the emotional burden.

After a year, check your heart. See how you have healed. Then—and only then—make the big decisions from a place of wholeness, not fragility.

Be careful of people who want to take advantage. When you are grieving, you are vulnerable. Protect yourself by holding off on sudden decisions and instead surround yourself with people who have your best interests at heart.

The Legacy Binder

If you are married right now, I want to give you a gift—one that could spare your spouse enormous pain if something happens to you.

Create a legacy binder.

This is a folder or binder—kept in a safe place—that contains everything your spouse would need to know if you died tomorrow.

Both of you should know exactly where it is and what is in it. This can also be stored electronically.

What goes in the legacy binder?

- Passwords for all bank accounts and online accounts
- Life insurance policy information
- Retirement account details
- Tax returns
- Social security cards and marriage and birth certificates
- Estate plan or living trust documents
- Instructions for how you want to be buried

- Wishes for how the children should be cared for
- Any other information that would lift a burden from your spouse

Review it together once a year. Update it as things change.

This is a beautiful gift. You will not be there to see your spouse receive it—but imagine being able to take away their burden before it ever arrives. Imagine giving them peace in the middle of grief.

Do not wait. You do not know which one of you will go first. Create the legacy binder today.

Rebuilding Trust With Money

If you experienced financial betrayal in your marriage, rebuilding trust is hard—like rebuilding trust after any kind of infidelity.

Get professional help. A counselor can help you unpack what happened, validate your feelings, and remind you that you are not crazy. Sometimes that is all you need—someone to tell you that your perspective is real and that you can be trusted.

Grieve your part in it. For financial infidelity to happen, someone was lying and someone was believing the lie. If you were the one believing, ask yourself: what about that season of my life made me willing to believe those lies? What would I do differently now?

Do an evaluation. What went well? What did not? What would you do differently if faced with that situation again? Making that decision now strengthens you for the future.

Part of that evaluation is looking at your boundaries.

Think of boundaries like a fence around your yard. Before the betrayal, maybe you had a short fence—or no fence at all. Anyone could walk in.

Now you know better.

It is okay to build a high wall at first. You have been hurt. That wall can protect you while you heal. But over time, start letting the wall down—first with yourself. Show yourself that you can be trusted. Did you pay a bill on time? Did you ask good questions? Did you stay within your budget?

Rebuild trust with yourself first. Then, slowly, carefully, you can begin to trust others again.

Faith in the Fire

What role does faith play in financial healing after loss?

Everything.

Prayer. Reading the Bible. Pouring out your heart to God. The Psalms are a great place to start—especially the laments, where David cries out in pain and grief.

God wants you to pour out your heart to Him. He can handle it.

Let God fill the void. Do not run to another person to fill it. Do not run to spending or substances or unhealthy relationships. Let God speak to you and heal you in His time.

He promises beauty for ashes. He promises to bind up the broken-hearted.

He saves those who are crushed in spirit.

Your garden may have burned down. But the soil is still good. And with God, you can replant.

Reflection & Replanting

1. If you have experienced divorce or loss of a spouse, what is one thing you are still grieving? What would it look like to release it to God?

____

____

____

2. What practical financial step do you need to take this week? (Open an account, run your credit report, create a budget, etc.)

____

____

____

3. Who is in your community? Who can you lean on during this season?

____

____

____

4. If you are married, do you have a legacy binder? What needs to be added to it?

____

____

____

5. What does "facing your front" look like for you right now?

____

____

____

Chapter 6 Mantra

Say this out loud:

I can rebuild wealth.
Wealth can be healed and regrown.
Beauty can rise from ashes.
I face my front.
God is still good, and I can still grow.

The fire does not have to be the end.

The soil is still good. You can replant.

In the next chapter, we will learn how to steward wealth when you are caring for others.

Chapter 7 - Caregivers

You Are Not God---and That Is Good News

What beliefs were planted in you about caring for others?

Maybe you grew up believing that good people sacrifice everything for their family---no matter the cost. Maybe you inherited the belief that asking for help is weakness. Maybe you were taught that your needs come last, always.

These beliefs take root early. And when you become a caregiver---for an aging parent, a sick spouse, or a child with special needs---those roots determine how you carry the weight.

Caregiving is one of the most loving things a person can do. It is also one of the heaviest.

Whether you are caring for an aging parent, a spouse with a chronic illness, or a child with special needs, you know what it feels like to carry the weight of another person's wellbeing on your shoulders. You make decisions. You manage doctors and insurance companies. You sacrifice your time, your energy, and often your money.

And somewhere along the way, you may have started to believe that you have to do it all. That if you do not hold everything together, it will all fall apart.

But here is the truth: you are not God.

You are not all-knowing. You cannot see the future. You are not limitless in your ability to give. And God does not expect you to be. He expects you to do what you can---and to trust Him with the rest. This chapter is about stewarding wealth beyond yourself---caring for others financially without losing yourself in the process.

What Caregiving Really Costs

People do not talk about the financial burden of caregiving. But it is real. There are the obvious costs: medical bills, prescriptions, equipment, home modifications, and hired help. But there are hidden costs too. There is the time spent on the phone---hours on hold with insurance companies, doctors' offices, government agencies.

My mother would sometimes spend one or two hours on a single call regarding by father's health, navigating systems that were not designed to be easy. That is time you cannot bill. Time you cannot get back.

There is the emotional cost of making decisions under pressure. Medical professionals, insurance companies, caseworkers---they all come at you with different options and different scenarios. You have to make a decision, sometimes in minutes, with incomplete information. And then a family member comes along later and asks, "Why did you do that?" But they were not there. They did not face what you faced. It is not fair to judge someone for a decision made in the heat of caregiving.

There is the career cost. Some caregivers reduce their work hours. Some quit their jobs entirely. Some pass up promotions because they cannot take on more responsibility. The lost income adds up over years.

And there is the cost to your own health. Relational and physical. Some pass up the opportunity to marry or delay it to care for their family. Caregivers who do not set healthy boundaries often burn out. Some get sick. Some pass away before the person they were caring for---because they gave everything and kept nothing for themselves.

Caregiving is costly. Acknowledge that. And then make a plan to protect yourself while you serve.

What I Learned Watching My Mother

When my father became ill, I watched my mother navigate one of the hardest seasons of her life. She handled the emotional weight. She made the healthcare decisions. She managed the finances. She sat on hold with institutions for hours. And she did it while grieving. But my mother's caregiving did not begin with my father's illness---and it did not end with his passing.

For decades my mother cared for a variety of people, including me, through sicknesses and hospitalizations. For years, she has also been responsible for her brother---my uncle---who does not live with her but depends on her for his medical decisions. Even while caring for my father, she was navigating a second layer of caregiving: communicating with doctors, making decisions on her brother's behalf, and relaying those decisions to family members in Nigeria.

Since my father passed, my mother's responsibility for her brother has only increased. She is the one who receives the calls from the hospital. She is the one who makes the hard choices. She is the one who explains those choices to family across the ocean who may not fully understand the American healthcare system.

I have had the privilege of supporting her in small ways. On some occasions, I have been by her side when she visited the hospital. When she traveled out of town, I stepped in as the contact person for his care. These moments gave me a window into the weight she carries---the phone calls, the decisions, the emotional toll of being responsible for someone else's wellbeing while still healing from her own loss.

Watching her has taught me something important: caregiving often extends beyond your immediate household. It can stretch across generations, across continents, across circumstances. And no one should carry that weight alone.

I did not handle the physical caregiving for my father---my mother, brothers and brother-in-law did much of that. My sister helped carry the mental and relational load. But I watched. And I learned.

One thing I learned from watching was the importance of having more than one person familiar with the system. In my family, we were blessed. I have brothers in the medical field who understood how hospitals work. I have another brother who runs a caregiving business and knows how to navigate services for families. My mother is never alone. And that has made all the difference.

After my father passed, I was honored to help my mother navigate the financial side. I still sit in on phone calls with her on occasion---calls to banks, to legal advisors, to financial institutions.

She trusts me to communicate calmly and clearly on her behalf. That is where I can serve.

Today, my mother is in a good place. She is still grieving---that does not end---but she has gotten her legs under her financially. She is making decisions on her own. And all her children contribute to support her.

Not everyone has a family like mine. But everyone can build a family.

Remember that the Bible admonishes us that believers, brothers and sisters in the Lord, are more a family than those with whom we share a DNA. Find people who can share the burden. Do life with them before you need them. We are better together.

Get in Your Parents' Business

There is a widow in financial trouble---and her children are unaware how dire her situation is. Her husband passed years ago and left her with what seemed like a decent amount of life insurance. She has been living off that money ever since. But she has no income. She does not work. And now the life insurance is almost gone.

You do not want to find out that your mother is eating cat food out of a can because she didn't tell you she ran out of money. You do not want to discover that your father is about to lose his home because he stopped paying the mortgage and did not tell anyone.

Adult children need to ask questions. After a certain age---especially if a parent has lost a spouse or is showing signs of slowing down---you need to get involved. Not to control them. Not to take away their dignity. But to partner with them and protect them.

Ask the big questions:

- Do you have a will? A living trust? Power of attorney?
- Do you have life insurance? Health insurance? Long-term care insurance?
- What are your wishes if something happens to you?

But also ask the everyday questions:

- How are you eating? What are you eating?
- Are you paying your bills? Are you paying them on time?
- Do you have enough money in your account to last the

month?

- Do you need to move in with us so you are not carrying this alone?

Show compassion. Show care. But ask.

You also want to protect your parents from scams. As people age and their mental sharpness declines, they become targets. Elderly people succumb to scams they never would have fallen for in their younger years. Get involved so you can protect them.

When Parents Do Not Want to Talk

In some cultures---including Nigerian culture---children do not ask parents about money. It feels disrespectful. It feels like overstepping.

But sometimes love requires us to overstep. Apply grace in wise doses with biological family and those in the faith.

If your parent does not want to talk about finances, approach them with all the love and respect you can. You may need to plant seeds over time---bringing it up gently, again and again, in different ways. It may take a year of conversations before they open up.

Try saying something like this:

"Mom, Dad---I am concerned about you. I want to be the best son or daughter I can be. I want to honor you. I want to honor your life and your legacy. I do not want to be blinded by my busyness to see when you are struggling. I want to make sure you are taken care of while you are alive, and I want to make sure your wishes are respected when you pass. Please allow us to have this conversation."

Do not try to cover everything at once. That is overwhelming.

Pick one topic at a time. And sometimes the best thing you can do is simply listen. Create space for them to talk. Record what they say if they are willing. Let them share at their own pace.

When they do share, do not react with shock or anger or judgment. If your reaction is negative, they will stop talking. Be calm. Be supportive. Say, "Okay. Now what are we going to do about that?"

Show them that telling you will not break you. Show them that you can handle it. That is how you build trust over time.

Dividing Caregiving Among Siblings

Caregiving is rarely divided equally among siblings or within a family.

And that is okay---because equal is not always possible. One sibling may live close by while another lives across the country. One may have more flexible work. One may have more money or disposable income. One may have more emotional capacity while another lacks mental bandwidth. The goal is not equal---it is fair. And fair means everyone contributes what they can.

Start by asking two questions:

First: What are your expectations for caring for Mom or Dad? Just listen. Do not judge. Let each sibling share what they think should happen.

Second: What are you able to contribute---financially, emotionally, physically? Again, just listen. Let each person be honest about their capacity.

Once you have heard from everyone, identify what actually needs to be done. Make a list.

Then look at the gaps---the things that need to happen, but no one has volunteered for.

Sometimes the answer is to outsource. If no one can provide the physical care, maybe you hire someone. Then the question becomes: how do we pay for it? Can we split the cost? Can it come from the parent's own accounts or insurance?

Outsourcing can be a gift. It allows you to simply enjoy your parent in the time you have left with them, instead of being exhausted by the physical work. If you can afford it, consider it.

Caring for a Child with Special Needs

Caregiving does not only mean caring for aging parents. Many families care for children with disabilities---and those families face unique financial challenges.

Parents of children with physical, behavior, mental or other disabilities often become fierce advocates. They navigate school systems, schedule endless appointments, fight for services, and learn to see past their own discomfort about their child's differences. It is exhausting work---and it never really ends.

One of the biggest questions these parents face is: what happens when I am gone? Who will care for my child? And how do I leave them money without disqualifying them from the government benefits they need?

This is where financial planning becomes critical. There are two tools every parent of a special needs child should know about: the Special Needs Trust and the ABLE Account.

A Special Needs Trust is a legal arrangement that holds money for a person with disabilities without affecting their eligibility for government benefits like Medicaid or Supplemental Security Income (SSI). You can put money into the trust during your lifetime or leave it to the trust when you die. A trustee---someone you choose---manages the money and makes sure it is spent appropriately on your child's needs.

An ABLE Account is a tax-advantaged savings account for people with disabilities. You can contribute up to $18,000 per year, and the money grows tax-free. The first $100,000 in an ABLE account does not count against the $2,000 asset limit for SSI. This means your child can save money without losing their benefits.

Many families use both. The ABLE account handles everyday expenses---things your child can access quickly. The Special Needs Trust handles larger amounts---inheritances, life insurance payouts, long-term planning.

If you have a child with special needs, please consult with a special needs financial planner or an attorney who specializes in this area. The rules are complex, and mistakes can cost your child their benefits. Organizations like the Special Needs Alliance and the Academy of Special Needs Planners can help you find a professional in your area.

And if you need respite care---a break from the day-to-day work of caregiving---look for services in your area. My own brother runs a caregiving company that provides support to families with children who live with neurodiversity and other disabilities. These services exist because caregivers need rest. The health of a caregiver is vital. Do not be too proud to use available services.

Protect Yourself While You Serve

Here is a hard truth: you cannot pour from an empty cup.

If you drain your savings caring for a parent, you may not have enough for your own household. If you neglect your health caring for a spouse, you may get sick yourself. If you give everything to a child with special needs, you may have nothing left for your other children---or for yourself.

Jesus said, "Love your neighbor as yourself." That command assumes you love yourself first. You cannot give what you do not have.

So set boundaries. Know your limits---financially, emotionally, physically. Decide in advance: this is the maximum I can contribute each month. This is how many hours I can give. This is what I will not sacrifice.

Make sure your own household is cared for first. Your spouse. Your children. Your own needs. Then give from the overflow---not from the reserve.

If the person you are caring for has their own resources---savings, insurance, benefits---use those first before dipping into your own. Allow them the dignity to contribute to their own care.

And please, take care of your health. Eat well. Sleep. Exercise. See your own doctor. Too many caregivers die before the person they are caring for because they poured out without ever refilling. Protecting yourself is not selfish. It is wise.

You Are Not God

I want to remind you of something important: you are limited. And that is okay. God created humans with limitations.

You cannot see the future. You cannot heal anyone. You cannot be in two places at once. You cannot give endlessly without running out.

I want to caution you: do not play God when it comes to caring for someone. The desire to care is loving and good. But when you act as if you know everything, as if you have unlimited ability, as if the whole weight of this person's life rests on your shoulders alone---you are carrying a burden God never asked you to carry.

It is healthy to admit your limitations. In fact, it is necessary. Because if you pretend you have no limits, something will break---your body, your finances, your mental health, your relationships.

Do what you are able to do. And then let go of the rest.

Prayer is not Plan B. It is the first thing you should do. Pray not just for healing, but for God's will to be done. Surrender to His goodness and His justice. Believe that He truly sees the future and works all things for good.

Put the burden of your loved one in God's hands. The weight that feels crushing to you is nothing in His hands. He is sovereign. He is good. And He can be trusted.

What About You?

If you are a caregiver, I want you to ask yourself some honest questions:

Am I carrying a burden God never asked me to carry alone?

Have I set financial limits on what I can give---or am I draining my own future?

Am I taking care of my own health, or am I neglecting myself?

Do I have a team---or am I trying to do this alone?

Have I had honest conversations with my aging parents about their finances?

If I have a child with special needs, do I have a plan for when I am gone?

Your answers matter. Caregiving is holy work. But it must be done wisely, or it will cost you more than you can afford to pay.

Replanting Your Beliefs About Caregiving

If you grew up believing that good people give until they have nothing left, it is time to replant that belief.

The new soil says: I can care for others without destroying myself. I can set limits and still be loving. I can trust God to carry what I cannot.

If you inherited the belief that asking for help is shameful, dig it up.

Plant this instead: two are better than one. Community is strength, not weakness. I was never meant to do this alone.

If you were taught that your needs do not matter, uproot that lie. The truth is: I am valuable. My health matters. My future matters. Caring for myself is not selfish---it is wise stewardship of the life God gave me.

Examine the beliefs that were planted in you about caregiving and money.

Keep the ones that produce good fruit. Uproot the ones that drain you dry. And replant yourself in soil that will help you---and those you care for---flourish.

Reflection & Replanting

1. Who are you caring for right now? What is the financial, emotional, and physical cost?

____

____

____

2. What boundaries do you need to set to protect yourself while you serve?

____

____

____

3. What conversations do you need to have with your parents about their finances?

____

____

____

4. Who is on your caregiving team? Who else could you invite to share the burden?

____

____

____

5. What burden do you need to surrender to God today?

____

____

____

Chapter 7 Mantra

Say this out loud:

God is good.
God has my family in His hands.
I can trust Him with their care.
I will do what I can and surrender the rest.
I am not God---and that is good news.
God uses my wealth for good.

Caregiving is holy work. But you were never meant to carry it alone.

In the next chapter, we will bring the journey full circle—and learn how to keep walking in financial freedom.

Conclusion

Don't Eat The Seeds

Every tree starts as a seed.

And every seed was once planted somewhere—in soil it did not choose, by hands it did not control. That is where your money story began.

Not with your first paycheck, but with the beliefs that were planted in you long before you understood what money was.

Throughout this book, we have examined those beliefs. We have dug into the soil. We have inspected the roots. And we have made a choice: to stay planted where we are, or to be transplanted into richer ground.

Now, as we come to the end, I want to remind you of everything you have learned—and leave you with one final truth that will determine whether your tree flourishes or withers.

The Seeds We Planted

We planted a seed for the caregiver—the one who carries the weight of another person's wellbeing. We learned that you are not God, and that is good news. You are limited, and that is okay. Do what you can, and trust God with the rest. Protect yourself while you serve. God is good, and He uses your wealth for good.

We planted a seed for those who walked through disease, divorce or death of a spouse—those whose gardens burned down. We learned that fire does not have to be the end. The soil is still good. You can rebuild wealth. Beauty can rise from ashes. Face your front. Keep moving forward.

We planted a seed for parents—those planting seeds in the next generation. We learned that more is caught than taught. Your children are watching. Let them see you give, save, and spend with wisdom. Teach them when you are at home, when you are on the road, when you are going to bed, and when you are getting up. You are building a legacy that will outlast you.

We planted a seed for the married—two becoming one, including with their money. We learned that you move as one or not at all. Pull up chairs at the same table. Have the hard conversations. Build together what neither of you could build alone.

We planted a seed for the single—building a foundation before the ring. We learned that you do not have to walk alone. Stewardship starts now, not after marriage. The habits you build today will follow you into every season of life.

And we planted a seed for the emerging adults—the roots of your money beliefs. We learned that you were planted somewhere, but you can choose new soil. The messages you inherited are not the messages you have to keep. You can be transformed by the renewing of your mind.

These seeds have been planted. Now the question is: what kind of tree will grow?

Your Money Tree

I want to leave you with a picture.

Imagine a tree. Your tree. It has been replanted in good soil—the soil of wisdom, stewardship, and faith. Its roots go deep. You water it with the truth of God's Word. Its trunk is strong. You submit to God's pruning. The result is branches that are heavy with fruit.

This is your money tree.

You may have grown up hearing, "Money doesn't grow on trees." Parents would say it when their children asked for something they could not afford. "What do you think—we have a money tree in the backyard? Go outside and pick what you need?" The assumption was that money trees do not exist. That wealth is scarce. That there is never enough.

But I want to tell you something: money does grow on trees. You have a money tree. The question is not whether you have one—the question is how you treat it.

Two Ways to Treat Your Money Tree

If you stay in the poverty mindset, here is what happens:

You pick a fruit from your tree. And instead of enjoying the fruit and saving the seeds, you eat the whole thing—core, seeds, and all. You consume everything. Nothing is left to plant.

Then you pick another fruit. And another. You eat them all the same way—seeds and all—until there are no more fruits left on your tree. But you are still hungry. So you start cutting the branches. You burn them for firewood. You sell them for quick cash. You suck the life out of your own tree until there is nothing left but a stump.

This is what the poverty mindset does. It consumes everything. It thinks only of today. It leaves nothing for tomorrow.

But if you have the wealth mindset, here is what happens:

You water your money tree. You tend to it. You let the fruits grow bountifully. And when you need something—when there is an emergency, when an opportunity comes, when life requires provision—you walk to your tree and pick a fruit.

You enjoy the fruit. You bite into it. You let it nourish you. But you do not eat the seeds.

You take those seeds and you plant them. You grow another tree. And another. And another. Your orchard expands. Your provision multiplies. Your children and your children's children sit under the shade of trees you planted.

This is the wealth mindset. It enjoys the fruit but protects the seed. It thinks beyond today. It builds for tomorrow.

When Someone Blesses You

This principle applies even when the fruit comes from someone else's tree. When God rains down a blessing today, save some for tomorrow.

Too often, people receive a blessing they were not expecting—a gift, a bonus, an inheritance, a tax refund—and they consume the whole thing.

Someone blesses you with a thousand dollars and you spend the whole thousand. You buy stuff. You spend it all to pay down credit cards.

Nothing is left. No seed is planted.

But with the wealth mindset, you see that gift for what it is: a fruit.

And every fruit has seeds inside.

So you receive the thousand dollars, and you enjoy some of it, or pay down debt—but you take two hundred and sow it.

You put it into your savings. You invest it in your education.

You add it to your freedom fund. You discipline yourself to eat only the fruit.

You plant a seed that will grow into something greater than the original gift.

This is how wealth multiplies. This is how generational blessings are built. This is how you honor the Giver by stewarding the gift.

The Way God Designed It

This is not a new idea. This is how God designed creation from the very beginning.

In Genesis, chapter 1, God created trees that bear fruit, and within each fruit He placed seeds. It is a cycle of multiplication built into creation itself. Seed becomes tree. Tree produces fruit. Fruit contains seed. Seed becomes tree again.

God could have designed it differently. He could have made trees that produce fruit with no seeds—fruit that is only for consumption, never for multiplication. But He did not. He built increase into the system.

When you eat the fruit but save the seed, you are partnering with how God designed nature, and money, to work. You are aligning yourself with His economy—an economy of multiplication, not scarcity.

When you eat the seed, you are working against the design. You are choosing consumption over creation. You are choosing today over tomorrow.

Don't eat the seeds

Let Others Pick From Your Tree

As your tree grows and your branches become heavy with fruit, something beautiful will happen: other people will come sit under your tree and find shade.

Let them.

Others will pick low hanging fruit from your tree.

Let them.

Your children will frequent your tree picking the best ripe fruit. Your family will pick. Your church will pick. Your community will pick. People in need will come to you because they see that your tree has fruit.

Let them.

Do not hoard your fruit. Do not build a fence around your tree and guard it with fear. A tree that no one can pick from is not a blessing—it is just a decoration.

Be generous. Let people eat. Give freely.

But as you give of your fruit, encourage others to plant the seeds. Every fruit that leaves your tree should leave seeds behind—seeds of love and abundance that you plant into people, seeds that grow into more trees, seeds that ensure your giving never runs dry.

This is sustainable generosity. This is wealth that lasts. This is stewardship.

What Will You Do Now?

We have reached the end of this book. Soon you will close these pages and step back into your everyday life—your job, your bills, your family, your responsibilities.

But you are not the same person who started reading this book.

You have examined your roots. You have chosen new soil. You have learned what it means to steward wealth in every season of life—as an emerging adult building habits, as a single person building a foundation, as a married person building unity, as a parent building legacy, as a divorced or widowed person rebuilding from loss, as a caregiver trusting God with the renovation—knowing that some seasons require you to hold the weight of another person's wellbeing while God does the rebuilding.

You have the tools. You have the truth. You have a new identity.

Now the question is: what will you do with it?

Will you go back to the old soil? Will you slip back into the old mindset? Will you eat the seeds and wonder why your tree never grows? Or will you tend your tree? Will you water it with wisdom? Will you enjoy the fruit but save the seeds? Will you build an orchard that blesses generations? The choice is yours.

A Final Word

Thank you for picking from the fruits of my tree to inspect the seeds in your fruit.

I do not take it lightly that you trusted me with your time, your attention, and your heart. These pages hold pieces of my story—my family, my struggles, my faith, my failures, and my victories. I shared them because I believe your story can be just as powerful. You have the ability to replant yourself. You have the ability to grow. You have the ability to produce fruit that feeds others and seeds that multiply for generations.

Mind your money thoughts. Protect your roots. Water your tree.

And whatever you do—don't eat the seeds.

Final Reflection

1. What is the most important thing you learned on this journey?

____

____

____

2. What old belief are you leaving behind?

____

____

____

3. What new truth are you carrying forward?

____

____

____

4. What is one seed you will plant this week—one action you will take to grow your money tree?

____

____

____

5. Who will you share this message with?

____

____

____

The Complete Mantra

Say this out loud:

I am confident. I am disciplined. I am focused.
I am a good steward of my wealth.
I can create wealth. I can use wealth for good.
I can rebuild wealth.
I can trust God with my family.
God is good. God uses my wealth for good.
I will enjoy the fruit but save the seeds.
I will plant for tomorrow while living today.
My tree will grow. My legacy will last.
I will not eat the seeds.

The book ends here. Your growth continues.

Go plant good seeds.

Resource Directory

Thank you for reading Plant Your Money Seeds.

I created complementary resources to support you as you begin applying what you learned.

They're designed to deepen your awareness and help you take your next steps with clarity and confidence.

Scan the QR code below to access complementary resources.

handinhandconsulting.net/plantyou rmoneyseedsbookresources

This directory is updated annually to include vetted professionals who align with Hand In Hand Consulting's values of stewardship, integrity, and service.

Categories include:

Certified Financial Planners

Investment Advisors

Insurance Specialists

Real Estate Agents

Mortgage Lenders

Estate Planning Attorneys

Tax Professionals

Life Coaches

Annual Resource Directory – subscription available for professionals: To be listed, visit handinhandconsulting.net/partners

References

Books Mentioned

- The Total Money Makeover* by Dave Ramsey
- The Automatic Millionaire* by David Bach
- Know Yourself, Know Your Money* by Rachel Cruze
- The Millionaire Next Door* by Thomas J. Stanley and William D. Danko
- Values over Valuables* by Harmon Kong
- The Prodigal Father* by Dr. Lawrence Olusegun Olayele

Scripture References (NKJV)

Psalms 1:1-3 "Blessed is the man who walks not in the counsel of the ungodly, nor stands in the path of sinners, nor sits in the seat of the scornful; but his delight is in the law of the Lord, and in His law he meditates day and night. He shall be like a tree planted by the rivers of water, that brings forth its fruit in its season, whose leaf also shall not wither; and whatever he does shall prosper."

Genesis 1 --- God's creation of time, space, matter, and the seed-tree-fruit cycle of multiplication

Romans 12:2 "And do not be conformed to this world, but be transformed by the renewing of your mind, that you may prove what is that good and acceptable and perfect will of God."

Deuteronomy 6:7 "You shall teach them diligently to your children, and shall talk of them when you sit in your house, when you walk by the way, when you lie down, and when you rise up."

Matthew 25:14-30 --- The Parable of the Talents

1 Timothy 5:8 "But if anyone does not provide for his own, and especially for those of his household, he has denied the faith and is worse than an unbeliever."

2 Corinthians 9:8 "And God is able to make all grace abound toward you, that you, always having all sufficiency in all things, may have an abundance for every good work."

Luke 16:10 "He who is faithful in what is least is faithful also in much; and he who is unjust in what is least is unjust also in much."

1 Peter 5:7 "Casting all your care upon Him, for He cares for you."

Habakkuk 2:2 "Then the Lord answered me and said: 'Write the vision and make it plain on tablets, that he may run who reads it.'"

Proverbs 16:3 "Commit your works to the Lord, and your thoughts will be established."

Joshua 7 --- The story of Achan

2 Kings 4:1-7 --- The widow's oil

1 Samuel 25 --- The story of Abigail and Nabal

Genesis 21:14-19 --- Hagar in the wilderness

About the Author

Foluke Olayele is the founder and CEO of Hand In Hand Consulting, where she helps individuals and families build confidence and clarity in their financial journey. Drawing on her Christian faith, Foluke guides her clients in aligning financial stewardship with purpose and identity.

Her approach blends practical wisdom with mindset renewal to empower others to walk in abundance and peace.

Foluke is a Nigerian immigrant to the United States who grew up in Los Angeles, California.

She holds degrees from UCLA and Pepperdine University and has built a career in the industrial safety industry before finding her calling in financial coaching.

She is a mother who has navigated divorce, rebuilt her finances, and become a millionaire through intentional stewardship.

She lives in Southern California with her son.

Connect with Foluke: - Website: handinhandconsulting.net

For coaching inquiries, visit: handinhandconsulting.net

If you desire to know the loving God who sees you --

email foluke@handinhandconsulting.net

Continue Your Journey

This book is just the beginning.

If you are ready to take the next step in your financial journey, Hand In Hand Consulting offers resources for every stage of life:

Free Resources - Download reflection guides and worksheets at handinhandconsulting.net

3-Day Mini But Mighty Money Reset to identify your emotional spending patterns.

Coaching Services - Money Clarity Session ---

A 60-minute 1-on-1 session to understand your numbers and name your vision.

Financial Freedom Plan --- Ongoing coaching to help you create a system for lasting peace.

Whether you are drowning in student loan debt, saving to buy your first home, or navigating money conversations in your marriage, you do not have to figure it out alone.

Visit handinhandconsulting.net to learn more.

Hand in hand,

Foluke Olayele

Made in the USA
Coppell, TX
22 February 2026

72076361R00077